WLE TRUE

CATAPULTING FROM COLDITZ
and other
Incredible Escapes

Chosen by JOHN L. FOSTER

Ward Lock Educational

ISBN 0 7062 4192 4

First published 1982

Set in 10 on 11½ point Times
and printed by
Ebenezer Baylis and Son Ltd
London Road, Worcester
for Ward Lock Educational
47 Marylebone Lane, London W1M 6AX
A Ling Kee Company

CONTENTS

ACKNOWLEDGMENTS

The editor and publishers would like to thank the following for their permission to reproduce copyright material: Collins for 'Thirteen Days Hidden in a Cupboard' from *Return Ticket* by Anthony Deane-Drummond, and 'I've Got to Get Out Tonight' from *Reach for the Sky* by Paul Brickhill; The Hamlyn Publishing Group Limited for 'Too Good to be True' by Anthony Richardson from *Wingless Victory*; 'Catapulting from Colditz' from *The Colditz Story* by P. R. Reid, reprinted by permission of Hodder and Stoughton Limited; Michael Joseph Limited for 'Farewell Campo 12' from *Farewell Campo 12* by James Hargest; Weidenfeld and Nicolson Limited for 'Escape from the Condemned Cell' by André Devigny from *Great Escape Stories* edited by Eric Williams.

I'VE GOT TO GET OUT TONIGHT

Paul Brickhill

―――――――――

As a young man, Douglas Bader lost both his legs in a flying accident. But doctors fitted him with artificial legs, and he taught himself to move about so freely that when the Second World War broke out he was again able to take up flying. He was a distinguished pilot and was promoted to the rank of Wing-Commander.

On one of his trips to France, however, his plane was badly damaged and he was forced to bale out. He was taken prisoner and put in a German hospital. He immediately started to make plans to escape and contacted some of the local French people to ask for their help. But before he could make detailed plans he was forced to act. For, one day, after being taken from the hospital to a nearby airfield, where some German pilots wanted to meet the legless English flyer, he returned to the hospital to be told that he was going to leave for Germany the following day.

―――――――――

A comatose form lay in the bed by the window and the room stank disagreeably of ether. Bader looked across. 'Who's that?'

'New boy came in while you were out,' Hall said. 'Sergeant pilot. Shot down yesterday. They've just taken his arm off. He's still under the dope.'

The door opened and a German soldier wearing a coalscuttle helmet came in and said in atrocious English: 'Herr Ving Commander, tomorrow morning at eight o'clock you vill pleased to be ready because you go to Chermany.'

The words seemed to hit Bader right in the stomach.

Hall murmured: 'Tough luck, sir. Looks like you've had it.'

Bader roused and said crisply: 'Well, I've got to get out tonight, that's all.'

He lurched over to the window and pushed it open. It seemed a long way down. He turned back and scowled round the room, austere with its board floor and five prim beds.

Sheets! Knotted sheets!

Each bed had an undersheet and a double, bag-type sheet stuffed in the continental style. He stumbled over to his bed and ripped the sheets from under the blanket. Need more than that! He clumped to the two empty beds and stripped them the same way. With a sudden idea he began ripping the bag sheets along the seams to get two out of each one. The tearing seemed to scream a warning to the Germans.

'Make a noise,' he hissed to Hall, and Hall started on a monologue in a loud American voice. Both were acutely conscious of the guard just outside the door.

'Know anything about knots?' Bader whispered to Hall.

'Not a sausage.'

He started knotting the corners together in an un-skilled double 'granny' with three hitches, jerking tightly to make them fast and hoping they would stay so when the test came.

The knots took up a lot of length, and when he had finished the 'rope' was clearly not long enough.

'Here, take mine,' Hall said.

Gently he eased the sheet from under Hall and took off the top one. When he had added them the rope still did not look long enough.

Bader went over to the bed of the sergeant pilot, who was breathing stertorously under the ether. Gently working the sheet from under him, he said: 'This is frightful, but I've just got to.'

'He won't mind,' reassured Hall. 'I'll tell him when he wakes up.'

Soon he had fifteen sheets knotted together, littered around the room, and prayed that no one would come in. He pushed the sergeant pilot's bed to the window, knotted one end of the rope round the leg and stuffed the rest under the bed. Then he straightened the white blankets on all the beds and climbed back into his own, sweating, heart thumping, praying that darkness would come before the guard.

Time dragged while dusk slowly gathered in the room. It was not quite dark when the door handle rattled, the door opened and a German soldier stuck his head in and looked round. Bader could not breathe. The guard muttered 'Gut Nacht,' and the door closed behind him.

Three hours to go. As long as no nurse came to see the sergeant pilot!

Weary eons of time seemed to have passed before a clock somewhere in the darkness of St Omer chimed midnight. The night was breathlessly still. He eased on to the edge of the bed, vainly trying to stop the creaks, and strapped his legs on. Then his clothes. Praying that the guard was asleep in his chair, he took a step towards the window; the boards creaked and the right leg squeaked and thumped with a terrifying noise. Hall started coughing to cover it up as, unable to tiptoe, he stumbled blindly across the floor. At the window he quietly pushed it open and leaned out, but the night was coal black and he could not see the ground. Picking up the sheet rope, he lowered it out, hoping desperately that it was long enough.

Holding the rope, Bader leaned his chest on the window-sill and tried to winkle his legs out sideways. They seemed fantastically clumsy. Uncontrollable. Sweating, he took a hand off the rope to grab his right shin and bend the knee. Then somehow he was through, legs dangling, hands clutching the rope on the sill. The terrible pain pierced his ribs again, making him gasp.

Hall whispered: 'Good luck!' It sounded like a pistol shot.

He hissed: 'Shut up.' And then, 'Thanks.' Then he started easing himself down.

It was simple. The legs rasping against the wall were useless, but the arms that had developed such muscles since the long-ago crash at Reading took his weight easily. He lowered himself, hand under hand, under sure control. Holding the sheets was no trouble and the knots were holding – so far. In a few seconds he came to a window and knew it was the room where he had drunk champagne with the Luftwaffe. He was horrified to feel that it was open, but inside it was dark and he eased his rump on to the ledge for a breather, hoping the doctor was not sleeping inside. Sitting there, breathing quietly, he looked down but still could not see the ground or whether the rope reached it.

Very gently his feet touched the flagstones and he was standing, dimly seeing that yards of sheet seemed to be lying on the ground.

'Piece of cake,' he thought, and moved a couple of yards on to the grass, cursing the noise from his legs. Warily he steered across the grass towards where the gates should be, hoping the mysterious Frenchman would be there.

Something loomed darker even than the night. The gates! Then a shock – they were closed. He got his fingers in the crack between and one gate opened easily a foot. He squeezed through on to the cobbled *pavé* of the road and instantly, immediately opposite, saw the glowing end of a cigarette. He stumped across the road and the cigarette moved, converging on him. It came to his side with a dark shadow behind it that whispered 'Dooglass!' in a strong French accent.

'Oui,' he said, and the shape took his right arm and

they moved off along the *pavé*. The town was like a tomb in which his legs were making an unholy clatter, echoing into the darkness. He could not see, but the silent shape seemed to know by instinct. A pressure on the arm and they turned right and stumbled on.

The Frenchman began muttering to him: 'C'est bon. C'est magnifique. Ah, les sales Boches.'

Bader thought how funny it was, walking through the curfew in enemy-occupied St Omer arm-in-arm with a stranger he would not even recognize by day. He began to giggle. The Frenchman said 'Ssh! Ssh!' but that only made him giggle more. The Frenchman started to giggle and then it was so grotesque, the two of them giggling and clattering down the street, that it grew into loud laughter mingled with the terror inside him that the Germans would hear. Slowly the pent-up emotion washed away and the laughter subsided.

They walked on – and on. Five minutes, ten – twenty. His right stump without the stump sock began to chafe. Thirty minutes . . . it was sore and starting to hurt. He was limping badly and the Frenchman made soothing noises like 'Not far now' in French. Forty minutes must have passed. The steel leg had rubbed the skin off his groin and every step was searing agony. Stumbling and exhausted, he had both arms hanging on to the Frenchman's shoulders. At last the man took his arms round his neck, picked him up, dangling on his back, and staggered along. In a hundred yards or so he stooped and put him down.

He led the way and Bader stumbled after him up a garden path. A doorway showed ahead, and then he was in a little, low-ceilinged room with flowered wallpaper, and a tin oil-lamp on the table. An old man and a woman in a black shawl got up from the chairs and the woman put her arms round him and kissed him. She was over sixty, Madame Hiècque, plump and with a lined, patient face. Her husband, spare and stooping, brushed his cheeks with a wisp of grey moustache. Fleetingly he saw his guide, remembering mostly the lamplight sheen on the glossy peak of a cap drawn low over the face and the glint of smiling teeth. The young man shook his hand and was off out of the door.

The old woman said gently: 'Vous êtes fatigué?'

Holding on to the table, he said 'Oui' and she led him with a candle up some cottage stairs into a room with a huge double bed. He flopped on it. She put the candle on the table, smiled and went out. He unstrapped his legs with enormous relief, stripped to his underclothes and slid under the bedclothes into a gloriously soft feather-bed.

A hand on his shoulder woke him about 7 am. The old man was looking down, smiling. He left a razor, hot water and towel. Bader freshened up and examined his stump, which was raw and bloodstained, terribly sore. No help for it. Just have to bear the pain. He strapped his leg on and went wincingly downstairs. Madame had coffee and bread and jam waiting, and while he ate she planted an old straw hat squarely on her head and went out.

Madame came back in great glee. 'Les Boches,' it seemed, 'sont trés stupides.' He gathered she had walked to the hospital and stood watching mobs of Germans running around searching the area. Great joke! In halting French he tried to make her understand that his presence was very dangerous to them. If they found him he, himself, would only be put in cells and then sent to prison camp, but the Hiècques were liable to be shot. He should leave them and hide.

Madame said: 'Non, non, non, non . . .'. The Germans would never find him here. That evening her son-in-law, who spoke English, would come and they would discuss things and get him to the Underground. She examined his right stump and produced a pair of long woollen underpants. Cutting one of the legs off, she sewed up the end and there was a perfectly good stump-sock.

At noon the familiar drone came overhead and they took him out into the shelter of the walled back garden. Yearningly he watched the tangled con-trails and saw tiny glints as twisting aircraft caught the sun.

Madame gave Bader cold pork for lunch and went out again to the scene of the crime. She came back hugging herself with delight. Convinced that Bader could not walk far, the Germans had cordoned off an area round the hospital and were running about like ants, searching every house. But nowhere in this area.

He felt like twiddling his thumbs as the afternoon dragged. Madame went out again to see the fun. About half-past five there came a terrifying banging on the front door and a chill swept through him. The old man jumped as though he had been shot, peered furtively through the curtain, turned and whispered 'Les Boches!'

He grabbed Bader's arm and led him towards the back door. Only at the last moment Douglas thought to grab his battledress jacket. Together they stumbled into the garden, moving as fast as the legs would let him. Three yards from the back door, against a wall, stood a rough shed, galvanized iron nailed on posts, covering some baskets, garden tools and straw. The old man pulled the baskets and straw away, laid him on his stomach, cheek pillowed on his hands, against the corner of the wall and piled the straw and baskets on top.

There was not long to wait. Within a minute he heard voices and then tramping feet by the back door. A vague kind of twilight filtered through the straw but he could not see anything. The boots clumped along the paved path to the shed. He heard baskets being kicked about. The straw over him started moving with a loud rustle.

Miraculously the footsteps retreated, diminishing down the garden path. Elation filled him.

The boots were coming back up the path. Suddenly

they clumped again into the shed, then stopped and rasped about a yard from his head. From his heart outwards ice seemed to freeze his nerves.

The baskets were being thrown around, the boots rasped on the paving, and then there was a metallic clang that mystified him. There was a movement in the hay just above and another clang. His eyes turned sideways, saw a bayonet flash down an inch from his nose and stab through the wrist of his battledress jacket to hit the stone floor. He knew what the clang was and guessed that the next stroke would go into his neck.

ESCAPE FROM THE CONDEMNED CELL

André Devigny

―――――

After being arrested by the Gestapo, on 17 April 1943, André Devigny, a member of the French Resistance Movement, was put in the condemned cell at Montluc prison, near Lyons, to await execution. At first, his position seemed hopeless. But with a pin given to him by a fellow-prisoner he learned how to pick the lock on his handcuffs. He then made himself a chisel by grinding the handle of his iron spoon and managed to remove some planks from his door, so that he could get into the corridor outside. Since his cell was high up in the building, he planned to escape through a skylight in the corridor out onto the roof. So he made himself a sixty-five-feet-long rope with strips torn from his bedding and clothing, reinforced with wire from his mattress, and grappling-irons from the metal frame which surrounded the electric light in the cell.

Devigny's plans were complete, when another prisoner, an eighteen-year-old boy called Gimenez, was put into the cell with him. If Devigny escaped, he knew that the boy would be shot for not raising the alarm. He decided there was no option but to invite the boy to join in the escape attempt.

―――――

Gimenez took the boards from me one after the other and stacked them away. In the half-light we could just see the faint, barred outline of the gallery rails; it was too dark to make out the cell doors on the other side. I put out my head and listened. Only the creaking of beds as

9

sleepers turned over, and occasionally a bucket scraping along the floor, broke the silence – that hostile silence against which we had to struggle for what seemed like a century.

For two long minutes I remained motionless. Then I pushed one arm out into the corridor, turned on one side, and crawled forward like a snake. I stood up cautiously. The light was on down below; but, as usual, its feeble rays were swallowed up in the vast gloom of the hall.

Gimenez passed me the light rope, which I at once took over to the latrines. It was followed by the rest of our equipment. I went back to the cell door to help Gimenez. We both stood there for a moment, listening. All was still. Slowly we moved towards our starting point.

I tied one end of the light rope round my waist – the end, that is, which had no grappling-iron attached to it. Three steps, and we were standing by the metal rod. The rope would pay out as I climbed; I left it coiled loosely on the ground. Gimenez braced himself against the wall and gave me a leg up. I stood on his shoulders, both hands gripping the rod, and tried to reach the edge of the skylight. I pulled myself up slowly, with all the strength I had. But it proved too much of an effort; I had to come down again.

The weeks of confinement I had undergone since my previous successful attempt must have sapped my strength more than I thought. We went back to the latrines to give me a few moments' rest. I inhaled deeply, waiting till I got my breath back before making a second attempt.

I had to get up there, whatever happened.

Jaws clenched, I began to climb. I got my feet from Gimenez's hands to his shoulders, and then to his head. My fingers gripped the metal rod convulsively. Somehow I went on, inch by inch; at last my fingers found the frame of the skylight, and I got my legs over the horizontal rod, which shook in its rings as my weight hung from it. I got round the ratchet supporting the skylight without touching it. I was sweating and panting like a man struggling out of a quicksand, or a shipwrecked sailor clinging desperately to a reef. Eyes dilated, every muscle cracking, I gradually worked my way through the opening. Then I stopped for a minute to get my strength back. I had managed to preserve absolute silence from start to finish.

A few lights twinkled in the distance. The fresh night air cooled my damp face. It was very still. Slowly my breathing became normal again. Carefully I put one hand on the gritty surface of the flat roof, taking care to avoid touching the fragile glass in the skylight itself; this done, I hauled myself up a little further and got my other hand into a similar position. With a final effort I completed the operation, and found myself standing upright on the roof, dazed by the clear splendour of the night sky. The silence drummed in my ears.

For a moment I remained motionless. Then I knelt down and slowly pulled up the rope. The shoes were dangling in their bundle at the end of it. I let it down again and brought up our coats. The third time I salvaged the big rope; it was a difficult job to squeeze it through the narrow opening.

Go slowly, I thought. Don't hurry. You've got plenty of time.

I unhooked the parcel and put it aside. Then I paid out the rope once more. We had agreed that Gimenez should tie it round his waist so that I could take up the slack and make his ascent easier. I waited a little, and then felt a gentle tug. I pulled steadily, hand over hand, taking care not to let the rope bear heavily on the metal edge of the skylight. We could not risk any noise. I heard the rods creaking under his weight; then, a moment later, two hands came up and got a grip on the sill.

Slowly Gimenez's face and shoulders appeared.

I bent down and whispered: 'Don't hurry. Take a rest.'

He breathed in the fresh air, gulping and panting.

My mouth still close to his ear, I said: 'Be careful how you pull yourself up. Don't put your hands on the glass.'

He seemed as exhausted as I was.

I untied the rope from my waist, and he followed suit. I coiled it up carefully, took a piece of string out of my pocket, and ran a bowline round the middle of the coil.

There we both stood, side by side, in absolute silence. Gradually my breathing slowed down to its normal rate, and I began to recover my strength. It was hard to get used to this immense, seemingly limitless space all around me. The glass penthouse (of which the skylight formed a part) stood out from the roof and vanished in darkness only a few feet away. I made out one or two small chimney-cowls here and there. The courtyard and the perimeter were hidden from us by the parapet. We could walk upright without being seen.

I felt the shingle grit under my feet at the least move I made.

I took a coil of rope in each hand and picked them up with great care. Gimenez did the same with the shoes and coats.

We stood there waiting for a train: it was five, perhaps even ten, minutes coming.

Gimenez became impatient. I was just about to move when the sound of a locomotive reached us from the distance. It grew louder and louder; presently the train steamed past on the nearby track. We managed to get ten feet before it vanished into the distance again. The stretch of line which runs past Montluc joins the two main stations of Lyons. As a result it carries very heavy traffic, which had hardly slackened off even at this stage of the war.

We had nearly reached the middle of the roof now.

We found ourselves standing by the far end of the penthouse. A little further on a second penthouse appeared, which stretched away towards the other side of the roof. My eyes were beginning to get accustomed to the dark. I could see the large glass dome above the penthouse; that meant we were standing above the central well. I thought then for a moment of our friends below in their cells: some asleep, lost in wonderful dreams; others, who knew of our plan, awake, awaiting in frightful suspense, ears straining for any suspicious noises.

We had advanced with extreme care, putting each foot down as lightly as possible, bent double as if the weight of our apprehension and of the dangers we had to face was too heavy to be supported. Gimenez kept close behind me. I could hear his slow, regular breathing, and glimpse his dark silhouette against the night sky. We had to wait some time before another train came to our assistance. But this time it was a slow goods train. It enabled us to reach our objective – the side of the roof opposite the infirmary – in one quick move.

We put down our various packages. I turned back and whispered to Gimenez: 'Lie down and wait for me here. Don't move.'

'Where are you going?'

'To see what's happening.'

Gimenez obediently dropped to his knees, and remained as motionless as the equipment stacked round him. I crept slowly round the corner of the roof, raised myself cautiously, and peered over the parapet. Below me I could see the stretch of the perimeter which flanked the Rue du Dauphiné. I lifted my head a little further, and quickly drew it back again at the sight of a sentry. He was standing in one corner near the wash-house. I had known he would be there; yet in my present situation he scared me nearly out of my wits.

Of course, he could not see me. I told myself not to be a fool.

I pressed my cheek against the rough concrete surface and slowly raised my head once more. Unfortunately, the wide shelf outside the parapet cut off my view of the part of the courtyard immediately below. As this was where we would have to climb down, it was essential to find a better observation-post.

But before moving I took another quick look at the soldier in the far corner. He seemed very wide awake. Soon a second sentry walked over to join him – probably the one who guarded the wooden barrack-block on the other side. I saw the glowing tips of their cigarettes. The lamps in the courtyard gave off so weak a light that the men themselves were mere shadows against the surrounding gloom.

Occasionally a twinkling reflection from buckle or bayonet hinted at their movements. I knew that the best way of remaining unseen was to keep absolutely still. If I had to move, it must be done as slowly as possible, with long and frequent pauses. It took me some time to get back to Gimenez, tell him to stay put, climb over the parapet, and crawl along the outer cat-walk till I was once more opposite the infirmary. A train passed by at exactly the right moment; I scrambled along as fast as I could to the corner of the wall. A loose piece of shingle, even a little sand going over the edge would have given me away. I would feel ahead with my hands, then slowly pull myself forward like a slug, breathing through my mouth.

In front of me the perimeter was clearly visible. Beyond it the tobacco factory and the buildings of the military court formed a broken outline against the horizon. Above them the stars shone out in a moonless sky. After a little I could just make out the roof of the covered gallery over which we had to pass. Gradually our whole route became visible. I spotted a familiar landmark – the fanlight of my old cell – and then, on the left, the workshop and women's quarters. Close by was the low wall between the infirmary and the courtyard. Soon, I thought, we should be climbing that wall. One room in the infirmary was still lit up; the light shone behind the wall in the direction of the covered gallery. I was, I realized, directly above cell 45, where my first few weeks of detention had been spent.

I wriggled forward inch by inch, so as to reach the outer edge of the cat-walk and get into a position from which I could observe the whole area of the courtyard. The two sentries were now out of sight round the corner of the block, smoking and chatting. I could see no one below me. The way was clear. My heart beat excitedly. A little further and I would be certain. My face against the rough surface, I peered cautiously over the edge.

I was horrified at the gulf stretching down below me; I could not help feeling that my rope must be too short.

Nothing was stirring. I examined every danger-point in turn – the shadowy corners by the wash-house and workshop, the women's quarters, the alley between the infirmary wall and the main block, the half-open doors leading from court to court, every conceivable hole or corner where a sentry might be lurking. Nothing. The cell windows were patterned on the façade like black squares in a crossword puzzle. Occasionally the sound of a cough drifted out from one or other of them. This, and the recurrent trains, alone broke the silence. Further down, on the left, some of the windows seemed to be open. The stillness was almost tangible.

Still I scrutinized the courtyard with minute care. Suddenly a dark shape caught my eye, in a corner near the door of the main block. I stared closely at it. After a moment I realized it was a sentry, asleep on the steps. The weight of this alarming discovery filled me with a sudden vast depression. How on earth were we to get past him? How could we even be certain he was asleep? How – in the last resort – could we surprise him without being seen?

At this point the sentry sat up and lit a cigarette. The flame from his lighter gave me a quick glimpse of his steel helmet and the sub-machine gun he carried. He got up, walked a little way in the direction of the infirmary, and then came back again.

Midnight struck.

It must have been the time when the guard was changed. The soldier passed directly beneath me, between the infirmary and the main block, and vanished in the direction of the guardhouse. Four or five minutes later his relief appeared. His footsteps crunched grimly over the cobbles.

A frightful inner conflict racked me as I studied his every movement, like a wild beast stalking its prey. We could not retreat. The way had to be cleared.

The sentry's beat took him away into the shadows at the far end of the court, then back to the main door, where the lamp shone for a moment on his helmet and the barrel of his sub-machine gun.

I watched him for nearly an hour, memorizing the pattern of his movements. Then I raised myself on knees and elbows, climbed quietly over the parapet, and returned to Gimenez.

He was asleep. I woke him gently. 'Time to move on,' I said.

He got up without making any noise. I was busy untying the knot of the string lashed round the big rope.

'All set now,' I whispered. 'As soon as a train comes, we'll lower the rope.'

I stood with one foot on the roof and the other on the cat-walk, the low parapet between my legs. This way I could control the rope with both hands and pay it out without it touching the edge. I left Gimenez to control the coil and see the rope was free from entanglements.

An eternity of time seemed to pass before the train came. At the first distant panting of the engine I began to lower away, slowly at first, then with increasing speed.

When I felt the reinforced stretch near the end passing through my fingers I stopped, and lowered the rope on to the concrete. Then I hooked the grappling-iron on to the inner side of the parapet. It seemed to hold firm enough. The rope stretched away into the darkness below us.

Gimenez would sling the parcels containing our shoes and coats round his neck, and follow me down when I gave him the signal. I knew that the moment I swung out from the roof into open space the last irrevocable decision would have been taken. By so doing I would either clinch my victory or sign my own death-warrant. While I remained on the roof it was still possible to return to my cell. Once I had begun the descent there was no way back. Despite the cool night air, my face and shirt were soaked with sweat.

'Hold on to the grappling-iron while I'm going down,' I told Gimenez. I took hold of his hands and set them in position.

Then I crouched down on the outer ledge, facing him, ready to go down the rope at the first possible moment, and waited for a train to pass. Gimenez leant over and hissed nervously in my ear: 'There's someone down below!'

'Don't worry.'

Then I looked at the sky and the stars and prayed that the rope might be strong enough, that the German sentry would not come round the corner at the wrong moment, that I would not make any accidental noise.

The waiting strained my nerves horribly. Once I began my descent there would be no more hesitation, I knew; but dear God, I thought, let that train come quickly, let me begin my descent into the abyss now, at once, before my strength fails me.

The stroke of one o'clock cut through the stillness like an axe.

Had an hour passed so quickly? The sentries' footsteps, echoing up to us with monotonous regularity, seemed to be counting out the seconds. There could not be so very many trains at this time of night.

Gimenez was showing signs of impatience. I told him to keep still. The words were hardly out of my mouth when a distant whistle broke the silence. Quickly it swelled in volume.

'This is it,' I said.

I shuffled back towards the edge of the cat-walk. Then, holding my breath, I slid myself over, gripping the rope between my knees, and holding the ledge with both hands to steady myself. At last I let go. The rope whirred upwards under my feet, the wire binding tore at my hands. I went down as fast as I could, not even using my legs.

As soon as I touched the ground I grabbed the parcel containing the second rope, and doubled across the courtyard to the low wall. I released the rope, swung the grappling-iron up, hauled myself over, and dropped down on the other side, behind the doorway, leaving the rope behind for Gimenez.

The train was fading away into the distance now, towards the station. The drumming of its wheels seemed to be echoed in my heaving chest. I opened my mouth and breathed deeply to ease the pressure on my lungs. Above me I saw the dark swinging line of rope, and the sharp outline of the roof against the sky.

I stood motionless, getting my breath back and accustoming my eyes to the darkness. The sentry's footsteps rang out behind the wall, scarcely six feet away. They passed on, only to return a moment later. I pressed both hands against my beating heart. When all was quiet again I worked round to the doorway, and flattened myself against it. I felt all my human reactions being swallowed up by pure animal instinct, the instinct for self-preservation which quickens the reflexes and gives one fresh reserves of strength.

It was my life or his.

As his footsteps approached I tried to press myself into the wood against which my back was resting. Then, when I heard him change direction, I risked a quick glance out of my hiding-place to see exactly where he was.

He did exactly the same thing twice, and still I waited.

I got a good grip on the ground with my heels; I could not afford to slip. The footsteps moved in my direction, grew louder. The sentry began to turn . . . .

I sprang out of my recess like a panther, and got my hands round his throat in a deadly grip. With frantic violence I began to throttle him. I was no longer a man, but a wild animal. I squeezed and squeezed, with the terrible strength of desperation. My teeth were gritting against each other, my eyes bursting out of my head. I threw back my head to exert extra pressure, and felt my fingers bite deep into his neck. Already half-strangled, the muscles of his throat torn and engorged, only held upright by my vice-like grip, the sentry still feebly raised his arms as if to defend himself; but an instant later they fell back, inert. But this did not make me let go. For perhaps three minutes longer I maintained my pressure on his throat, as if afraid that one last cry, or even the death-rattle, might give me away. Then, slowly, I loosened my bloodstained fingers, ready to close them again at the least movement; but the body remained slack and lifeless. I lowered it gently to the ground.

I stared down at the steel helmet which, fortunately perhaps, concealed the sentry's face; at the dark hunched shape of the body itself, at the sub-machine gun and the bayonet. I thought for a moment, then quickly drew the bayonet from its scabbard, gripped it by the hilt in both hands, and plunged it down with one straight, hard stroke into the sentry's back.

I raised my head, and saw that I was standing immediately below the window of cell 45. Old memories fireworked up in my mind: hunger and thirst, the beatings I had suffered, the handcuffs, the condemned man in the next cell, Fränzel spitting in my face.

I went back to the doorway, near the infirmary, and whistled twice, very softly. A dark shape slid down the rope. It creaked under his weight. I went to meet him. Gimenez climbed the low wall, detached the light rope with its grappling-iron, passed them down to me, and jumped. In his excitement, or nervousness, he had left our coats and shoes on the roof. At the time I said nothing about this. Clearly his long wait had depressed him; he was shivering all over. He gave a violent start when he saw the corpse stretched out near our feet.

I clapped him on the back. 'You'll really have something to shiver about in a moment. Come on, quick.'

Our troubles had only begun. We still had to cross the courtyard in order to reach the wall between it and the infirmary. Then there was the roof of the covered gallery to surmount, and, finally, the crossing of the perimeter walls.

I carried the rope and the fixed grappling-iron; Gimenez had the loose one. We doubled across to the wall. It was essential for us to get up here as quickly as possible. The light left on in the infirmary was shining in our direction, and a guard could easily have spotted us from a first-floor window of the central block as we made our way towards the inner wall of the perimeter.

Gimenez gave me a leg up, and I managed to reach the top of the wall and hang on. But I was quite incapable by now of pulling myself up; all my strength had drained away. I came down again, wiped my forehead and regained my breath. If I had been alone I should in all probability have stuck at this point. As it was, I bent down against the wall in my turn, and Gimenez got up without any trouble. I undid the bundle of rope and passed him the end with the grappling-iron attached. He fixed it securely. Then I tried again, with the rope to help me this time. Somehow I scrambled up, using hands, knees and feet, thrusting and straining in one last desperate effort. Gimenez lay down flat on his belly to give himself more purchase, and managed to grasp me under the arms. Eventually I made it.

My heart was hammering against my ribs and my chest felt as if it was going to burst. My shirt clung damply to my body. But there was not a minute to lose. We coiled up the rope again and crawled along to the covered gallery. From here it was a short climb up the tiles to the ridge of the roof. We had to hurry because of that damned light; once we had got over the other side of the roof we were in shadow again.

Unfortunately I made a noise. Two tiles knocked against each other under the sliding pressure of my knees. Gimenez reproved me sharply.

'For God's sake take care what you're doing!' he hissed.

'It wasn't my fault –'

'I haven't the least desire to be caught, even if you have!'

Since this was a sloping roof, we only needed to climb a little way down the far side to be completely hidden. If we stood upright we could easily see over the wall. Soon we were both crouching in position at the end of the covered gallery, our equipment beside us.

I was not acquainted with the exact details of the patrols in the perimeter. When I went out to be interrogated, I had observed a sentry-box in each corner, but these were always unoccupied. Perhaps the guards used them at night, however: it was vital to find out. We already knew that one guard rode around and round the whole time on a bicycle; he passed us every two or three minutes, his pedals squeaking.

We listened carefully. Gimenez was just saying that the cyclist must be alone when the sound of voices reached us. We had to think again.

Perhaps there was a sentry post at each corner of the square, in the angle formed by the outer wall. If this turned out to be so, it would be extremely difficult to get across; nothing but complete darkness would give us a chance. That meant we must cut the electric cable, which ran about two feet below the top of the inner wall, on the perimeter side.

I half rose from my cramped position and took a quick look. The walls seemed much higher from here, and the lighting system enhanced this impression. A wave of despair swept over me. Surely we could never surmount this obstacle?

From the roof it had all looked very different. The yawning gulf had been hidden. But the perimeter was well lit, and the sight of it – deep as hell and bright as daylight – almost crushed my exhausted determination.

I craned forward a little further. The sentry-box below on our left was empty. I ducked back quickly as the cyclist approached. He ground round the corner and started another circuit. A moment later I was enormously relieved to hear him talking to himself; it was this curious monologue we had intercepted a moment earlier. He was alone, after all.

Behind us rose the dark shape of the main block. We had come a long way since ten o'clock. Another six yards, and we were free. Yet what risks still remained to be run!

Little by little determination flowed back into me. One more effort would do it. Don't look back, I thought. Keep your eyes in front of you till it's all over.

Bitter experience had taught me that over-hastiness could be fatal; that every precipitate action was liable to bring disaster in its train. Gimenez was eager to get on and finish the operation, but I firmly held him back. I was as well aware as he was of the dangers that threatened us; I knew that every moment we delayed increased our risk of recapture. I thought of the open cell, the rope we had left hanging from the wall, the dead sentry in the courtyard, the possibility of his body being discovered by a patrol or his relief. Nevertheless, I spent more than a quarter of an hour watching that cyclist. Every four or five circuits he turned round and went the other way. We were well placed in our corner: he was busy taking the bend, and never looked up. We were additionally protected by three shaded lights fixed on each wall. All their radiance was thrown down into the perimeter itself, leaving us in shadow. We could watch him without fear of discovery.

Three o'clock.

Gimenez was becoming desperate. At last I decided to move. Holding the end of the rope firmly in one hand, I coiled it across my left arm like a lasso. With the other hand I grasped the grappling-iron. As soon as the sentry had pedalled past, I threw the line as hard as I could towards the opposite wall. The rope snaked up and out, and the grappling-iron fell behind the parapet. I tugged very gently on it, trying to let it find a natural anchorage. Apparently I had been successful; it held firm. A strand of barbed wire, which I had not previously noticed, rattled alarmingly as the rope jerked over it. After a little, however, it was pressed down to the level of the wall.

I gave one violent pull, but the rope did not budge. It had caught first time. I breathed again.

'Give me the other hook,' I muttered to Gimenez. I could feel him trembling.

The cyclist was coming round again now. I froze abruptly. For the first time he passed actually under the rope. When he had gone I threaded the rope through the wire loop and we pulled it as tight as we could. While Gimenez held it firm to prevent it slipping, I knotted it tightly, and fixed the grappling-iron in a crevice on the near side of the parapet. In my fear of running things too fine I had actually over-calculated the amount of rope necessary; over six feet were left trailing loose on the roof. That thin line stretching across the perimeter looked hardly less fragile than the telephone wires which followed a similar route a few yards away.

I made several further tests when the cyclist was round the other side. I unanchored the grappling-iron on our side, and then we both of us pulled on the rope as hard as we could to try out its strength.

If the truth must be told, I was horribly afraid that it would snap, and I would be left crippled in the perimeter. When I pulled on it with all my strength I could feel it stretch. One last little effort and the whole thing would be over; but I had reached the absolute end of my courage, physical endurance, and will-power alike. All the time the cyclist continued to ride around beneath us.

Four o'clock struck.

In the distance, towards the station, the red lights on the railway line still shone out. But the first glimmer of dawn was already creeping up over the horizon, and the lights showed less bright every moment. We could wait no longer.

'Over you go, Gimenez. You're lighter than I am.'

'No. You go first.'

'It's your turn.'

'I won't.'

'Go on, it's up to you.'

'No,' he said desperately, 'I can't do it.'

The cyclist turned the corner again. I shook Gimenez desperately, my fingers itching to hit him.

'Are you going, yes or no?'

'No,' he cried, 'no, *no!*'

'Shut up, for God's sake!' I said. I could not conquer his fear; I said no more. Still the German pedalled round his beat. Once he stopped almost directly beneath us, got off his machine, and urinated against the wall. It was at once a comic and terrifying sight. As time passed and

24

the dawn approached, our chances of success grew steadily less. I knew it, yet I still hesitated. Gimenez shivered in silence.

Abruptly, as the sentry passed us yet again, I stooped forward, gripped the rope with both hands, swung out into space, and got my legs up into position. Hand over hand, my back hanging exposed above the void, I pulled myself across with desperate speed. I reached the far wall, got one arm over it, and scrambled up.

I had done it. I had escaped.

A delirious feeling of triumph swept over me. I forgot how exhausted I was; I almost forgot Gimenez, who was still waiting for the sentry to pass under him again before following me. I was oblivious to my thudding heart and hoarse breath; my knees might tremble, my face be dripping with sweat, my hands scored and bleeding, my throat choked, my head bursting, but I neither knew nor cared. All I was conscious of was the smell of life, the freedom I had won against such desperate odds. I uttered a quick and thankful prayer to God for bringing me through safely.

I moved along the top of the wall towards the courthouse buildings, where it lost height considerably. I stopped just short of a small gateway. Workmen were going past in the street outside, and I waited a few moments before jumping down. This gave Gimenez time to catch up with me.

At five o'clock we were walking down the street in our socks and shirt-sleeves – free men . . . .

THIRTEEN DAYS HIDDEN
IN A CUPBOARD

Anthony Deane-Drummond

Anthony Deane-Drummond was a parachutist. In 1941 he was captured, following a raid in Italy, and managed to escape across the Swiss border. In September 1944 he was again captured, after being parachuted into the region around Arnhem in Holland where bitter fighting was taking place. It was not long, however, before he began looking for a way of escaping. He made careful preparations, but his plan went awry and he was forced to spend thirteen days hidden in a cupboard.

The game was up and I was a prisoner again. Once more I went through the indignity of being searched by the enemy, but on this occasion I at least had no weapons to surrender. I had to let go my sten gun and pistol while swimming across the Rhine.

No longer was I a free man and the anticlimax suddenly made me remember my hunger, and how every bone and muscle in my body ached for rest. Wearily, so wearily, I was marched down the road to the Company HQ, watched by sleepy-eyed Germans from slit trenches dug into the verge.

We stopped at a farmhouse and I was shown into a room, after pushing aside a black-out blanket which had been nailed over the doorway. Inside, a hot aroma of unwashed bodies, the acrid stench of stale German tobacco smoke and seasoned sausage combined to stifle my nostrils. A hurricane lamp turned low gave the only light, and in the gloom my smarting eyes could now see gently-heaving bodies wrapped up in greatcoats lying all over the floor, with mounds of equipment taking up every vacant space. The only sounds were wheezes and snores except for the faint noise of a conversation in German coming from a next-door room.

One of my escort of three pushed by and, after mumbling what I took to be swear words, woke up one of the prostrate Germans. He turned out to be an NCO and was soon kicking the other bodies into life, who grunted in a dialect I did not understand, and then stood up and stretched. A piece of paper passed hands and I was off again out of the house with three new guards to Battalion HQ which was about a mile away.

This time everything was much more orderly, and after a German sentry had examined the piece of paper carried by my escort, we went down some steps into a cellar whose roof had been chocked up with large baulks of timber. A clean-shaven, middle-aged German subaltern sat at a table with a lamp on one corner. He motioned me to sit down and said in broken English:

'I must to you questions ask. You will answer.'

'Oh.'

'Your name, please?'

I told him.

'What day you jumped?'

'I can't say.'

'How many more are you?'

'I can't say.'

His eyes seemed to bulge a bit behind his glasses, and an angry flush spread up his neck.

'OK. You no speak. We will see.'

He ended with some instructions in German and I was shown outside into the back of an open Volkswagen car, in which I was driven along the road towards Arnhem.

We crossed the Rhine using the main bridge for which so many lives had been sacrificed. I could see many marks of the bloody fighting which had taken place as we threaded our way in and out of shell holes and burnt-out German tanks. Smoke was still coming from the ruins of the buildings on the north side of the river.

We sped on through deserted streets to the outskirts of the town and stopped outside a newly-built church which had sentries posted all round it. I was told to get out and wait inside. There I found the church full of newly-captured prisoners of war standing in little groups everywhere. In one corner I could see a few officers, none of whom I knew, and I learned from them that the division was now fighting inside a small perimeter round Oosterbeek, a suburb about three miles from the centre of Arnhem.

In another corner I saw Lance-Corporal Turner and three others who had shared the lavatory[1] with me. They, too, had been captured that morning in various places not far from where I had been taken. All touch had been lost while swimming across, and Turner had been caught while trying to find a hiding-place in a farmhouse. Daylight had come before he had reached a point anywhere near the railway bridge.

We all looked pretty scruffy in that church. I had a five-days' growth of beard, not having had a chance to shave, and many were like me. All had the slightly haggard and drawn look of soldiers who have been without sleep, and seen their best friends die, not knowing when their own turn might come. Some were rummaging in their pockets or haversacks for any crumbs left over from the once-despised 48-hour concentrated ration that we all carried. Many were lying down full-length on pews fast asleep, snoring away with mouths slightly open and heads twisted at any angle.

As the morning drew on, the air in the church became warmer, and more and more of us lay down where we were on the hard tiles and went fast asleep. I followed suit after checking that all doors were guarded and there was no way of getting out.

The Germans still gave us nothing to eat and by midday we were all getting very hungry and thirsty. Some men I spoke to asked me if I could get the Germans to do something about it.

After some argument I managed to get hold of an officer who could speak some English and in a mixture of two languages I told him we expected to be given food within an hour, or else I would see that his name was remembered after the war when the time came to deal with the war criminals who disobeyed the Geneva Convention.

He became quite angry and spluttered:

'You can all think yourselves lucky to be alive and you will get food when it pleases us. Anyhow, what do you know about Geneva Conventions?'

'You would be surprised,' I replied, 'but food we must have, and it is your responsibility to provide.'

'Let me tell you, Herr Major, I have just received orders to march you all to a prison near here run by the SS. I am sure they will feed you.'

With a glint in his eye, he turned on his heel, and five minutes later we were on the march with guards on all sides. For two miles we went through the suburbs and saw very few civilians, one or two of whom were brave enough to wave and smile as we went by.

Eventually we arrived at a house on the outskirts of Arnhem in another suburb called Velp. This was used as a prisoner-of-war cage and was guarded by an under-strength company of fifty-five men. It was a typical large suburban house, about twenty yards back from the main road and with exactly similar ones on either side. Two monkey-puzzle trees stood on the front lawn.

Inside the house were about five hundred all ranks of the Division, whose spirits were high except for the ignominy of being prisoners. Here I met Freddie Gough, Tony Hibbert, and many others. I learned all their news and told them mine. The Germans fed us on tins of lard and coarse brown bread, but we were not fussy and I wolfed my share down. I had not had a really square meal since leaving England, my last being breakfast on the 17th, and today was the 22nd. What months it all seemed and yet it was only five days.

I heard that the bridge had been captured by the Germans soon after dawn on the 21st, when nearly all the original defenders were killed or wounded, and all ammunition had been expended. Colonel Johnny Frost had himself been wounded, and for the last twenty-four hours Freddy Gough had been in command. For three days and nights this gallant force had held out against overwhelming odds, including tanks, which came up and gradually knocked down or set on fire every house that was being used for the defence. Some of these tanks had been stalked on foot and blown up with grenades. Fighting patrols had gone out every night to drive the Germans out of houses which overlooked the bridge. Deeds of heroism were done which are matchless in the history of the British Army, but received little publicity at the time because nobody returned to tell the tale. The Division had been ordered to hold the bridge for forty-eight hours until the arrival of the Second Army. It had been held for seventy-two hours by six hundred men, but unfortunately to no avail.

We now realized what a failure the whole operation had been but we still hoped that the Division could hold on where it was and provide the Second Army with a bridgehead from which the advance could continue. Many were our speculations on what was happening to the rest of our units still fighting, but our hearts were heavy and we could not help thinking about ourselves and our present plight.

I remember the latrines inside the house were hopelessly inadequate for the numbers of men, and some deep trenches had been dug at the bottom of the garden at the back of the house. In this garden were growing carrots and onions, and we quickly dug these up and distributed them on the basis of half a carrot or onion per head. It took some of the hunger away.

All this time I was looking for ways out of the house or garden. I was determined to escape and not be a prisoner longer than I could help. Now would be the time and it would be infinitely easier than later on.

Some of the officers were already saying that they would leave trying to escape till they arrived at the German prison camp. It would all be 'laid on' there. It is so easy to put off action till tomorrow and all this sort of talk was so reminiscent of my experiences in Italy. I told everybody I saw that their one and only chance of getting away would be before they left Holland. The further they went back along the evacuation channels, the more difficult would escape become. I think they believed me, but most of them could not see any possible way out with any hope of success. When I started looking over the whole house and the garden there were many smiles cast in my direction. It was not possible to get away, they said, they had already been over the place with a fine-tooth comb. The trouble was that most of them were numbed by the anticlimax of being prisoners, and they did not realize that small though the chances of getting away were at the moment, they would be better now than at any future date.

I reasoned that the cage would only be temporary and would last as long as the Division did. From all accounts this would not be long, so one solution would be to hide up in the house itself till the Germans left and then to get out. Again it was just possible that the Second Army would continue their advance through the Division's bridgehead, and then the area would be liberated.

I could not see any way to escape that gave a better than fifty-fifty chance of success, so I looked everywhere for a hiding place that would hold me for two or three days. The only possible place seemed to be a wall-cupboard in one of the ground floor rooms, which had a flush-fitting concealed door. The whole door was covered with the same sort of wallpaper as that of the rest of the room, and was difficult to see except on close examination. The cupboard was about four feet across, twelve inches deep, and about seven feet high. Its interior was divided horizontally by adjustable shelves, but by removing the shelves I was able to stand inside in tolerable comfort. Fastening the door was a problem. The cupboard was fitted with the normal type of mortice lock let into the thickness of the door, with a keyhole on the outside complete with key. By unscrewing the lock, and turning it back to front, the keyhole came on the inside of the door and I was able to lock myself in. A piece of wallpaper, torn from another part of the room and pasted over the outside keyhole, helped to conceal the cupboard's presence.

The next job was to lay in a stock of water and food. All I had was my waterbottle, and I found an old two-pound jam jar that I also filled up. A one-pound tin of lard and half a small loaf of bread completed all the provisioning I could do. Some of the officers very kindly offered to give me their waterbottles, but I refused. They would need then for their own escape, which, I reminded them, they must try to make or be a prisoner for the rest of the war.

Little did I think that I would be confined to my cramped little cupboard for thirteen days and nights before getting out. I thought that the limit of my endurance would be reached after three or four days, because I did not start off in the best condition for an endurance test. The Germans came round on the evening of the 22nd to take all names, and in order to avoid a record being taken I started standing in my cupboard. Pole squatting is, I believe, a time-honoured sport in the USA. I cannot recommend cupboard-standing to anybody who wants to try out something new. I stood first on one leg, then on the other; I leaned on one shoulder and then on the other. There was no room to sit down because the cupboard was too shallow. I managed to sleep all right, although occasionally my knees would give way and would drop forward against the door, making a hammer-like noise. Every bone in my body ached, and I felt quite light-headed from lack of food, water and rest.

The day after I locked myself in the cupboard the Germans turned the room into an interrogation centre. Every officer and man going through that cage was first interrogated in the room where my cupboard was. It was certainly an interesting experience, which I believe had never been rivalled, though I scarcely appreciated its uniqueness at the time. We in the army had always been instructed that if ever we were made prisoner, the only information that we should give would be our army number, rank and name. The Germans knew this, of course, but tried every guile to get more information. The usual trick was to pretend that they were filling out a card for the Red Cross, and ask a series of innocuous questions until the prisoner was at ease, when a question of military importance would suddenly pop up. It was a surprising thing to me that very few officers or men gave only their number, rank and name. Almost everybody gave a little additional harmless information, such as the address of their parents or wives, or whether they were regular soldiers or had been in the TA before the war.

Only two gave away military information. One was a captain in the Glider Pilots, and another was the batman to a company commander of the leading battalion of relieving Second Army. This battalion had assaulted across the Rhine opposite the division's perimeter in order to allow the successful withdrawal of the division. These two men, who shall be nameless, gave all the information they knew or were capable of giving. Luckily neither was in possession of any real military secrets and no great harm was done, except to my pride. The officer talked so much, and seemed so promising a source of information, that he was given lunch just in front of my cupboard door. What agonies of mind and tummy! To hear all this coming out, and to smell what seemed to be a delicious meal only a few yards from my hiding place. I nearly burst out of the cupboard on several occasions to stop the wretch giving information. I think I would have done so if he had started to say anything serious. Luckily he did not know much and I kept my peace and exercised self-control over my mental anguish.

The questioning went on for several days, four or five I think, and by night the room was used as sleeping quarters for the German guard. I had no chances to get out at all, but as I had lasted so far, I resolved to try to remain a little longer. My luck must come to my rescue. It had always done so up till now.

Little by little I eked out my rations of water and bread. Four mouthfuls of water every four or five hours and just a bite or two of rye bread. The water was the chief shortage, and after nine or ten days I could not eat any more bread because my mouth was so dry. For the benefit of the curious, I was able to direct my urine through a paper funnel into one corner of the cupboard where there was a gap in the floorboards to allow some pipes to pass down to the cellar. It interested me to see that I continued to pass water in spite of drinking practically nothing. I did not feel the need to do anything more solid during the whole time, perhaps because there was nothing in my tummy. My system started to function again quite normally as soon as I started to eat when I got out. My only legacy was a series of bad boils, followed by styes which persisted for about a year afterwards.

It was now 5 October, 1944, and the thirteenth day of my voluntary confinement. My water was nearly at an end, and the cramp in my muscles hurt acutely most of the time. Patience and caution were now finished and I told myself that I would have to make an attempt to escape that evening or fail in the effort.

The room outside my cupboard was still full of Germans but provided no new prisoners came in that evening there would be a good chance of the whole guard leaving the room empty for half an hour or so at sunset. On the previous evening they had all cleared out of the room and hung over the garden wall adjoining the main road outside my window, to watch the passers-by in the twilight. I suppose it is a worldwide habit to come out of the houses on a warm evening for a breather before going back inside for the night. The only thing that might spoil it would be new prisoners; but there had not been any last night, so with any luck I would get away tonight.

I slowly shifted my weight from one leg to the other, and leaned alternately on my right shoulder and then my left. By now, shifting my position had become almost automatic, and no longer required any thought or even consciousness. My mouth was dry as a bone, but I had already had both my dawn and midday mouthfuls. My evening one was not due for another two hours yet. Tonight I would take three mouthfuls of water. What bliss this promised to be!

It was due to get dark about 7.30pm or 8pm, and I hoped the room would clear by about 7pm. I would then have to hide up in the bushes near the house for an hour, till it was really dark, before it would be possible to move round to the back of the house and get away.

The minutes slowly crept by while I waited anxiously, my ears taut for the sound of the Germans leaving the room. Occasionally one of them would go in or out, but I could hear snores from two or three having an after-lunch nap. At about 6 o'clock I pulled on my boots and smock and gathered all my equipment. Dressing in that cupboard was a work of art, and to avoid making a noise it was three-quarters of an hour before I was ready. While I was dressing I heard two Germans stumble out of the room, but I was fairly certain that there were one or two more. Sure enough, by their grunts and the bumping of boots on the floor, I heard two more get up and go out talking about a *fräulein*.

The time had come. Cautiously I unlocked my door. There might still be the odd squarehead making up arrears of sleep. I opened the door an inch and had a quick look round. Damnation take it, there, not six feet away, was a solitary German soldier sleeping with his hands crossed over his tummy and his mouth wide open. As I had to walk across the floor and open the big french windows, which were both noisy operations, I decided to give him another half-hour.

A few troops came clattering into the building with a couple of girls, all talking at the tops of their voices. I heard them go upstairs and enter the room directly over my head, and they soon had quite a merry party going with songs and a gramophone, and an occasional girlish giggle or scream. I was in luck. They were probably not expecting any prisoners tonight, and if the noise increased as the wine flowed I should have no worries about covering up squeaks as I opened a window.

The noise upstairs woke my sleeping soldier after about twenty minutes, and he got up and walked out. This was my chance and, taking a couple of mouthfuls of water, I gently pushed the door open again. This time the room was empty. I could see the guards lining the garden fence on the main road and not ten yards away. My plan was to get the window open and then wait for a lorry or tank to go by before slipping out and into the shrubs growing almost under the sill. The Germans would be most unlikely to look back towards the house when anything interesting was passing.

I was in luck and no sooner had I opened the windows when a large truck went clattering by. This was my cue, and I was quickly out and had dropped into the shrubbery. My luck held good on the thirteenth day in that Dutch cupboard.

I quickly crawled into the bushes where it was thickest at the corner of the house, and concealed myself as best I could with dead leaves. From where I was I could see eight or ten of the guard idly leaning against the garden fence a few yards away and could hear them chatting unconcernedly about the war in general and their sweethearts at home. From the windows above came occasional strains of gramophone records and the semi-delighted, semi-frightened squeals from the not-too-particular girls.

Notes
[1] During the house-to-house fighting at Arnhem.

FAREWELL CAMPO 12

James Hargest

Brigadier James Hargest was the highest-ranking British officer to escape in either of the two world wars. He was captured in Africa in November 1941 and was imprisoned in the British Generals' Camp near Florence. At first, the attempts to escape from that camp centred on trying to get over the walls, but eventually it was decided that the only way to escape was to dig a tunnel, and that the best place to start tunnelling from was the chapel.

Progress was very slow and laborious, and sometimes it seemed impossible to get on. The rock appeared to be quite solid and beyond the scope of our tools to deal with; but we learned much as we went. Caused either by the castle's great weight, or by an earthquake, the rock was always found to be fragmented if we persevered long enough. First a thin line would appear on the surface of the stone, indicating the place to work on. Much scratching with the knife would outline a crack that could be developed. Alternately scraping and clearing away the debris and cutting into the very tight clay above and below permitted the placing of a lever under the point of the stone; then, by dint of much worrying, the stone would loosen and perhaps fall out. Most of the rocks were triangular, nearly always with the point facing the workers, making the freeing process more difficult still. Sometimes the outgoing relief would pour water over a rock in the hope that it might disclose a crack not otherwise discernible; but the advantage was offset by the resultant mud which stuck to one's clothes and boots, and would have made detection easy in the event of a sudden appearance before an Italian, so we dropped the practice.

In the chapel we found a five-ton lifting jack which we sometimes used to put pressure under a stubborn rock; but that meant digging a hole in the floor to get the necessary length, and was rarely worthwhile. Our difficulties were principally caused by the lack of space in which to work levers, and the need for quiet. Each group of watchers was sure that the others were noisy and endangered the scheme. We found from practice that the sound of voices or the dropping of a bucket did not carry; but a heavy blow with the trowel or an iron bar reverberated all round the walls and up to the tower. When we came near the battlements where the sentries were overhead we used only the knife.

Our pace was slow. Some weeks we made only a very few inches; in some we made as much as three feet. Every Sunday Neame went down and measured the dimensions and the incline, making any recommendations he believed necessary. He devised an excellent inclinometer by getting Boyd to make a v-shaped apparatus, which he put into the bank horizontally. The top of the v was dead level, while the lower arm was shaped at an angle of one in eight. On this were nailed two pieces of cane which when at rest were swung into the v, but when needed could be opened out and used as sights. Someone held a marked stick upright at the working face and by sighting along it Neame could check the rate of incline to an inch. It worked so successfully that when we had reached the wall our incline was exact – we had gone down four feet.

By Christmas Day, after four months' work, we had travelled nearly twenty feet, and to reward the helpers among the officers and men we opened the workings for inspection in pairs. They were all suitably staggered at the scale of the undertaking. Most of them had thought we were a few elderly gentlemen full of enthusiasm but rather harmless as miners; but after this inspection they realized we were in earnest. The size of the rocks we had brought up impressed them. Our work achieved a new status.

The art of watching was perfected, and we brought everything down to a sort of drill. In the morning one of the servants – generally Collins – did a quick survey of the whole castle to see that there were no Italians about. This could not be done by an officer, who might have found it difficult to explain his being up so early in the day. Collins would report to the chief watcher who then placed sentries in the bathroom and bedroom respectively, while Collins went down to the dining-room to be ready to assist. Then the workers waiting in one of the bedrooms in their working clothes were summoned and, proceeding to the lift well, were allowed through and the panel replaced. Before they went down the shaft the signal buzzer was tested. After that they were free to work.

The watchers knew from practice what to expect and when. At half-past seven an NCO came in by the small gate and put out the light above the cloister steps. Then he opened the door of the courtyard. This called for one buzz; three buzzes meant that he had entered the court-yard. At seven forty-five the new guard relieved the old in the yard beyond the white wall, and a close watch was kept to see that the officer of the day did not enter our yard. At nine o'clock a soldier brought the milk into the kitchen by the small gate. During the five minutes he was there the workers were on one buzz. On certain days the laundry came, and on Saturday mornings at eight-thirty the shopping sergeant brought in the weekly flowers for Stirling to put into vases for Sunday's service and for the tables. On Sunday morning the three or four Roman

Catholics were taken to church at seven-forty-five, and we arranged that they were always ready and standing near the main gate. So it went on. We knew the habits of nearly every one of the sentries and just what they would do. Some found a patch of sun to stand in; some came down to the end of their beats and talked to their comrades; some read their letters; some just dozed. The ones we disliked were those who stood right opposite the bathroom window without moving, compelling the miners below to reduce their work by pushing the knife in and cutting out small bits – a very slow job.

We had many alarms – in fact few shifts passed without one. On many days they were serious. The gate would suddenly be approached by a carabiniere escorting a workman bringing in his tools to start on some job. This would necessitate the workers staying below or seeking a chance to slip out unseen. Sometimes an officer would come into the castle unexpectedly and just hang about, to our acute discomfort; sometimes a carabiniere would turn up from nowhere and appear to direct his attention on the very spot he was most unwelcome. One thing always intrigued me – the fact that for several hours every day for over six months all of our gaolers in the castle precincts were under the closest observation without being aware of it. And yet they were highly nervous of us. Nearly every night there was a search in some part of the castle. The living-rooms, the kitchen, the bathrooms, all came in for frequent scrutiny. Sometimes we would see them in the garden late at night turning over the refuse or poking about among our growing plants; but we never left anything there to arouse suspicion. All our efforts were bent on lulling them into apathy.

With the New Year our plans began to take a definite form and our preparations were pushed on. We hoped to complete the tunnel in mid-March and settled on March 20th as the earliest date we could leave. My hip was troubling me – tunnelling was not the best activity for it – and I applied to have it X-rayed and treated. I had to go down to a hospital in Florence for the X-ray and on each occasion I persuaded the driver to go by a slightly different route, enabling me to mark down road junctions and piazzas. From the top of the Quarries we could pick out these points, and we were eventually able to choose a first-class route from the castle to the railway station. I had massage in my room. It used to amuse me that the Italian masseur should work on me so painstakingly to fit me for my job in the tunnel. The cramped position in the heat, alternating with the chill of waiting at the shaft, was the real cause of my trouble.

In late January a dampness in the rock, which we knew must be the result of seepage from a water table, told us we were close to the outer wall. Timbering was necessary and Boyd and Miles set to work. While it was in progress Stirling and I used our shift to widen a short length as a bypass for up and down traffic. There was a division of opinion over this and over a later bypass; but on the last night they justified their construction. Sergeant Bayne, our electrician, carried the light along the wall beside us as required, and during the whole period not a bulb was broken.

We drove on until there could be no doubt that we were under the battlements; then we worked upwards by taking away the top and treading it underneath our feet. On the second day we found what we sought, the hard base of the wall – huge, square blocks of stone joined together by very hard concrete. They made an excellent roof, and we travelled along under it easily and safely for almost six feet, and beyond it for another two feet, when we were actually outside the limits of the battlements.

The next thing was to find just how far we were below the surface. We knew that we had fourteen feet of cover inside; but the ground fell away steeply and we had no means of being certain. It was imperative that we should drive upwards to within easy distance of the surface. Equally important was it that we did not approach it too rashly and risk a subsidence before we were ready to go out. While the other two shifts cleared up the tunnel and made another 'sitting-out' place under the wall itself, Boyd and Miles, assisted by Ranfurly, made and put in place what proved to be a very satisfactory device. The excavation beyond the wall was two feet wide. In this they placed three pieces of sawn timber on either side of the new upward shaft, with a gap of about four inches between each, and pieces of timber above each one as a ceiling. As progress was made the ceiling pieces were removed one at a time, some soil gouged out and the piece replaced. By this means we always had a firm roof and there was no danger of subsidence. As the shaft was pushed upwards other pieces of sawn timber were fitted inside and as they took the strain of the roof they were screwed into the outer uprights without noise. So each day the shaft ascended, very gingerly, but safely and almost noiselessly.

The next problem was to find the exact distance necessary. Neame solved this by taking a hollow stair-rod, sharpening one end and driving it ahead. To do this meant noise, and noise was dangerous under the sentries' very feet; so every three or four days a diversion was created in the driveway or in the courtyard. Heavy timber-sawing, the men playing football in the confined area, much bumping of the wall against the battlements, were all part of the scheme. When the sentries were nicely placed the General would drive his curtain-rod upwards, until one day daylight appeared. On measurement it was disclosed that we had nineteen inches to go in the total upward shaft of seven feet. From then onwards the greatest care had to be taken; but at last Boyd reported that the surface was only five inches away – easy cutting distance when the moment came. A ladder was fixed in position to facilitate the climb, the roof was reinforced and packed tight against pressure from the top. All was ready.

At the end we had one scare. There was a torrential downpour of rain. A regular river flowed down the tunnel forming a lake. Two of us went down and made a sump to hold as much as possible, and to place timber so that the water ran rather than dropped. In a few days the shaft dried out again.

Final preparations were pushed on. Kits were overhauled and everything possible was placed in the chapel where it was reasonably dry and safe from search. We knew that discovery there meant discovery everywhere. Food necessities were computed and chocolate and compressed tablets were in demand. Miles and I suffered a severe loss at this time. With the exception of broken fragments we had never allowed ourselves the luxury of eating chocolate, but stored it away in our cache until we had accumulated ten pounds. We used tins, each holding several pounds, and sealed the lids with adhesive tape. One night I brought mine up and opened it, to find that the whole lot had become mildewed and quite uneatable. There was nothing for it but destruction and at once I began to feed our stoves with it. In a few minutes the whole of the top flat reeked with the stench of burning chocolate. I was fearful that one of the guards would come in to investigate; but nothing happened and when Miles came up to bed the smell was dying down. Fortunately at this time I received several large tins of chocolate from my wife and was able partially to replenish our stocks.

We settled our routes and as a corollary the rough date of departure. De Wiart and O'Connor adhered to their plan of walking to the frontier, while the remaining four of us decided to go from Florence by train to as near the Swiss frontier as we could. We planned for speed. Apart from anything else we did not want to take a large amount of food. The walkers, on the other hand, had to take all the food they could carry. Their proposed two hundred and fifty mile walk more or less fixed the earliest date we could set off, for as they would have to live mainly out of doors, sheltering by day and walking by night, it was desirable that we should allow the spring to advance as far as possible to give them the advantage of the warmer weather. We decided that we would make March 20th zero day, and that we would leave on the first suitable night after that. To us a suitable night meant a wet one, preferably a windy, wet one. Heavy rain was essential to keep the sentries overhead in their boxes, and wind would assist in deadening the noise. As we all had our own ideas on suitability we agreed to hand the responsibility over to Neame, whose decision would be final.

Each night now I packed and unpacked my kit – a cheap little Italian suitcase Howes had given me; and almost every night I dressed in my room. In the kit I placed only Italian articles – soap, towel, shaving gear, scarf, spare underclothes and pyjamas. Food was to be restricted to two eggs, bread and cheese, and some food tablets. In the pockets of my raincoat I carried chocolate and some milk tablets, both English. My aim was to appear as a workman cleanly but carelessly dressed, going away to a new job equipped for the journey by a faithful wife. Miles was to go as a carpenter, Boyd as a workman and Combe as a commercial traveller. I would wear my jacket and cap, a green shirt Ranfurly gave me, a cheap tie Howes got from one of the boys, and heavy black boots, with my raincoat over my arm. I used to pay special attention to the set of collar and tie and to maintaining a certain facial expression.

As we intended going out through the tunnel entrance in heavy rain, we could expect copious mud and we all provided ourselves with overdress. I had an out-sized pair of pyjamas to pull over my clothes, including the raincoat, and a large handkerchief to tie over my cap to keep it clean. We had soft outer material to keep our boots clean and to reduce the noise. Some sewed up large felt overshoes; I slipped two felt soles under my boots and held them in place by two pairs of huge socks which protected my trouser-legs as well. We each had sufficient money and a map, and most of us had compasses.

We also had our identity cards. Over these, G.-P., our official artist and map-maker, rose to superb heights from which the fact clearly emerged that if he had not chosen to be a respectable major-general he might have had a successful career as a forger. Sketching and painting being his hobbies he was allowed a fairly good assortment of brushes, fine pens, paper, inks and colours. After we had obtained possession of a real Italian identity card he did not seem to have much trouble in matching the paper and copying the crest, stamp-markings, printed lines, and the signature of the issuing official. He spent hours mixing inks to get exact shades, and improvising stamps. Somehow he managed to procure special glasses which made the fine work possible.

We thought photographs would stump him; not a bit of it. For his weekly gramophone recitals it was necessary to buy records, and by a queer chance he discovered that the artists' photographs in the catalogues were the exact size of, and printed on similar paper to, those on identity cards. He sent for further catalogues and set up a small committee to choose likenesses. The results could not have been better – all six of us seemed to have more or less of a counterpart in German or Italian opera. They found me a celebrated German tenor, and G.-P. gave him my moustache more painlessly than I cultivated his right-hand hair-parting.

I called myself Angelo Pasco, after my old friend the fish-merchant in my native town of Invercargill; there was no chance of my forgetting it, and it was easy to pronounce. I came from Bologna, and you could see that

I was a bricklayer if you looked inside my case and saw trowel and plumbline lying on top.

To provide six identity cards was a long and arduous task. Before they were all ready even G.-P.'s happy disposition showed signs of strain; but they were six perfect replicas – it was impossible for the lay eye to tell the counterfeit from the original.

Miles had acquired a useful tool – a pair of pliers. One day he came to me with the news that a workman had left his pliers on the ground a little distance from his job. By that time we were no mean snappers-up of unconsidered trifles. Miles carelessly threw an old gardening sack over them and after the man departed we hurried them into hiding.

The next matter of importance, and it was very important, was the 1.30 am check. Every night the officer on duty, accompanied by a sergeant, came round our rooms and saw us all in bed, the servants as well. We could not expect to leave before nine o'clock, which would only give us four and a half hours' start. On the other hand, if we could evade this check we would not be missed until eleven in the morning at the earliest. We decided to use dummies. As a preliminary, Neame protested against the practice of the inspecting officers of coming right into our rooms; he insisted on their staying in the doorway and using their torches from there. After weeks of squabbling we got them used to this. Then as spring approached we applied for protection against mosquitoes, and nets were put up, great canopies completely covering each bed and reducing the rays of the torches to impotence.

Then we concentrated on our dummies. They were little masterpieces – all of them. Each had to be different and required different materials. Boyd was grey-haired, O'Connor and Combe fair, I dark and Miles and Carton bald. We persevered to such an extent that we produced tolerably good likenesses. I let my hair grow, and when

Howes cut it we stuck it on a handkerchief saturated with glue, not overlooking my bare spot on top. We fixed the handkerchief over a stuffed balaclava and sewed on an ear and the job was complete. Sometimes when we made up the bed it was difficult to believe that I was not really in it. Each week we had a small exhibition of dummies in bed, everyone interested being invited to throw in suggestions.

The last piece of rock was removed early in March. We were ready. All that was necessary was the suitable night, and we settled down to a period of waiting.

On Sunday, March 28th, it rained hard. As the day advanced we made ready. There was, of course, a certain amount of tension, and when at church service we found that G.-P. had included the hymn 'Through the night of doubt and sorrow onwards goes the pilgrim band' we were all a little moved. Right up till seven-thirty we thought there were great possibilities; but with night the rain eased and Neame cancelled preparations. Needless to say there were divergent opinions; but we had agreed to abide by his decision, and there was never any question of the wisdom of this.

Monday morning was fine; but as the day advanced clouds came over and by six o'clock it was raining hard, a silent rain, but very close to what we needed. I was on my bed resting about 7.30 pm when Neame looked in and said: 'I think you had better dress, Jim; it looks as though tonight will be a good one.'

At once we got to work and in a very few minutes I was ready. Ranfurly had reserved some sandwiches and hard-boiled eggs for each of us, and at the last I opened a bottle of rum which Stirling and I had kept for this occasion for over a year. I filled six two- or three-ounce medicine bottles, one for each man. There was also room for a small bottle of wine in my case.

Then came the hardest moment of the whole adventure: saying goodbye to Howes. For three years we had been together, in England and in the east. We had fought together; on all my leaves, however short, I had taken him. In the Greek and Cretan campaigns he had never left me for one moment, no matter how weary he was, and in our last fight he had shared my slit trench. He was a big, quiet young fellow who inspired confidence; in Vincigliata every officer and man liked and respected him. Of course he wanted to come with me; I would have given much to take him; but the risks were great and the chances of success so small that I did not feel I had a right to endanger him. So we said goodbye. War is hard in its goodbyes.

Dinner was a quarter of an hour earlier that night and we sat down all together for the last time, some of the boys mounting guard to prevent surprise. While we were dining Neame and Ranfurly passed through the hole into the chapel, Neame to see that all was right in the tunnel, Ranfurly to pull down the timbering at the far end and cut away the remaining earth up to the surface. He took the long knife and made a perfect job.

We were all waiting rather tensely, trying to conceal it beneath the veneer of small talk, when the last alarm came through from Vaughan's room: 'Officer coming'. We six escapees took up our cases and fled upstairs through the living-rooms. It was only an NCO making his round of the battlements. We trooped back to the dining-room. Things ran smoothly from then onwards. We said our goodbyes lightheartedly and one by one filed into the lift-landing and slid for the last time through the panel into the chapel porch. I was fourth man and when I got in the first three had disappeared down the shaft. Ranfurly was sitting, naked except for a pair of shorts, at the head of the shaft, and when I went to shake hands he said: 'For heaven's sake don't touch me, I'm just one greasy slimy mess from head to foot.'

Taking out those last five inches of mud had been a dirty business.

I found Neame sitting in the bypass. He reported that all was well. He had a shaded light there, and I could see Boyd's legs disappearing up the ladder. Each of us had a special task once we appeared on the surface. John Combe went first carrying his suitcase, a stout rope and a blanket. The blanket he spread on the ground to act as a carpet to avoid obvious marks a sentry could see when daylight came. The rope was to be hitched round a post on the top of a stone wall just down the hillside from the battlements. It was our last obstacle, five feet high on the uphill side and about ten feet on the downhill or road side. The rope was to steady us; we could hang on to it while descending. A huge iron gate about twelve feet high opened on to the road. As we had never seen it used in all the time we had been there we had no reason to hope that it might not be locked. Once over, John was to help Miles, who was then to be his assistant on the road. Miles, second man up, was to take a measured three-ply board reinforced for strengthening, to be used as a lid for the hole when the last man was out. Boyd was next and had just his kit. He was to get on to the road and act as scout while the rest came over.

I was number four and in addition to my suitcase had the hooked rope we always used for haulage and a sandbag full of pine needles and soil. I pushed the case up ahead of me, and dragged the sandbag up with my free hand – not easy in that confined space with mud oozing out from every side. When I emerged I had a shock. Instead of the darkness we had expected a couple of concealed lamps made it almost as light as day. Had an Italian been on that side he must have seen each of us as we came up. As it happened, the light certainly made our exit easy.

It was a tremendous experience. Not even the need for action could suppress the wave of exultation that swept over me. Here was the successful achievement of a year of planning and seven months of toil. I remember thinking, with a new kind of awareness, that whatever the immediate future held, at this moment I was alive and free. I have never been able to recapture in retrospect the fullness of that moment.

I put down my case and sandbag and passed the rope back into the shaft, hook downwards. A tug, and I began hauling up. Carton's large pack apeared. I unhooked it and fished again, this time for O'Conner's pack. All this was according to plan and I had hauled in and was waiting for a head and shoulders to appear when a whisper came up: 'The rope'. A bit surprised, I tried again; up came two walking sticks – I hadn't heard about them. De Wiart came surprisingly easily. As he surfaced I placed his pack on the stump of his left arm and off he went. O'Connor, following, disappeared into the darkness. I threw the carpet back down the shaft and clamped the board over the hole. It fitted perfectly and stood my weight as I pressed it down. I emptied my bag of pine needles on it and smoothed the surface. I even found a few stones and some chickweed to give it a natural appearance. The last job was to level off any remaining footmarks. Then, taking up my case, rope and empty sack, I decamped. It was exactly half-past nine.

They were all waiting at the foot of the little wall. We had had unexpected good luck, as the door to the road was not locked, and we passed through. I gave my rope to Miles, who cached it along with the other one in a place already chosen, not too conspicious, yet not too well hidden. When our flight was discovered we hoped that they would be found and give the impression that we had come over the top. We wanted to keep the secret of the tunnel as long as possible. Once through the door we found sufficient shadows to make the going safer. We began crossing the road. John, finding the door difficult to close, slammed it; the noise seemed to shatter our freedom.

We filed down through the wet woods in complete darkness, then across a fence into an olive grove. Thick brambles made the terraces difficult to negotiate; but we got down somehow without noise. Half-way down to the deep valley we were making for we stopped and hid our overclothes and my sandbag in some bushes. Six hundred yards lower down a roadway ran at right angles to our path. Here we said goodbye to O'Connor and de Wiart, who were using this as a starting-point for their long walk. We shook hands, and the darkness swallowed them up.

The rain had stopped, and we had no trouble in seeing our way downhill to a bridge above a mill, where we came on a tarred road. We threw our overshoes into the swollen stream. I felt terribly dirty, and seemed to be mud all over, so I soused my suitcase in the running water and cleaned off the worst of it. Then we set off on our six-mile tramp. The road offered no obstacles, we knew it so well from observation, and we tramped along it like a police squad in pairs, our heavy boots making a tremendous noise. It was the first time for months we had walked on a road unaccompanied by a guard, although I don't think we gave much thought to that at the time.

Once we got on to the lower ground nearer the city we began to meet people carrying torches or on lighted bicycles. We were a little tense at first; but no one took any notice of us and we soon became accustomed to them. We were dressed in very heavy clothes because we felt certain that if we succeeded in reaching the mountains near the frontier we would find snow and might have to sleep out in it. In addition we wore our greatcoats and before long we felt the heat and perspired like oxen. For some reason Miles and Boyd, who were leading, cracked on a very fast pace that seemed unnecessary and even dangerous. I caught them up and suggested slowing down as we had three hours from the start in which to do six miles, and it would be preferable not to arrive too early and too hot. They were afraid that we might miss our route, and wanted some time in hand. As it was, we arrived at 11.35pm. After a little careful reconnaissance, we went boldly into the huge hall of the station.

The ticket gate was at the far end, guarded by carabinieri and railway officials. We did not stay together but moved about separately to get the lie of the land. I wanted to see whether I drew any special attention, so took up a position close to some soldiers in the middle of the great hall; but neither they nor anyone else looked at me or my dirty boots, so I gained fresh confidence and ceased to be afraid of being detected through my dress.

We drifted outside and met in the shadow, Boyd going off to buy three third-class return tickets to Milan. In a few moments he returned rather perturbed. In response to his request the ticket clerk had asked a question or told him something, and Boyd had fled. We thought it could be nothing more serious than instructions about changing at Bologna, so Miles went over and bought the tickets without further trouble. Combe who was better dressed travelled second-class and bought his own ticket. The waiting was trying. To relieve the monotony we walked about the streets in pairs, coming back at intervals to see if there was any alarm. At about twelve-thirty we sauntered through the gates, It was quite simple. Adopting the slowish gait of an elderly workman I walked up and, looking each official in the eye as I reached him, passed safely through.

Then began a long wait. The train did not come in until 1.45am. It was to have left at 12.35am. Contrary to report, Fascism could not even run the trains punctually for us. All that time we walked about the cold, wet platform, afraid to sit down in case we sat on something forbidden – there were no regular seats. When the train arrived it was crowded to the doors, and the chances of getting aboard seemed remote. The seething crowd on the platforms surged towards the doors in solid masses, preventing anyone from alighting. I saw a new technique in train-boarding. Men and women ranged themselves along the platform opposite the compartment windows; a man would heave his lady up until she got a hand-hold which enabled her to go through the window. Then she reached down and hauled in the baggage which the man held up to her, afterwards taking his arms and pulling him up and in. We were well separated by this time and I had no one to haul me in. I determined that if anyone was left behind it wasn't going to be me, and tucking my bag safely under my arm I charged in. I don't know how I managed it, but eventually I got one foot on the step and the crowd behind did the rest, depositing me well in the corridor with Boyd not far behind. All this was done to the accompaniment of shouts, curses, and fierce arguments, in none of which I took part; but I was on board, I did not ask for more.

The Italians are wonderful people. At one moment they can hurl piercing diatribes at each other; at the next they are smiling and all politeness. In five minutes they were laughing and teasing and making room for each other like happy children. My only discomfort was due to the fact that the man next to me, not six inches from my face, was the carabiniere in charge of the carriage. After a while he began to talk to me. I ignored him, but he spoke again. I bent over and said in whisper such as I've often heard deaf people use: 'I'm sorry, but I am very deaf.' This was in Italian and probably very bad Italian, though I had practised hard; but it was effective and he left me alone.

The train was fast and we did the forty-five miles to Bologna in an hour, arriving at 3 am. The slow train to

Milan was due to leave precisely at that time, but actually it was twenty minutes past five before we got away. Another weary wait on a cold platform without any seats. Our efforts to find a refreshment buffet were fruitless. Once when the others were seeking food and I was watching the luggage, a policeman came up and asked me if all the bags were mine. I said they were and he walked off. Several people asked me about platforms or trains, but my chief anxiety was the delay. It was growing lighter and our features would become easier to distinguish. We had hoped to be in Milan by six o'clock and at Como by eight; we seemed to be stuck here indefinitely.

When the train did come in the scrimmage was fiercer than at Florence. By this time I had learnt from experience and, putting my head down, drove in, using my elbows on all who came alongside. By this method I got on to the step and mounted to the top; but then disaster overtook me. Someone clutched at my poor little suitcase and tore it out of my hand, leaving me only the handle. I had to make a quick decision – to retrieve it or leave it. I decided on the former, and kicking my legs clear I dropped straight down on the crowd struggling to mount the high steps. The cursing reached a high standard; but I found my bag and butting ahead with it climbed up again. This time I was further along the corridor. I could see Miles's tall figure at the other end and Boyd about six feet behind me. We ignored each other.

I repaired the handle of my bag with a boot-lace, and standing with my back to the outside wall held it behind my neck so that it would not be trampled on. My legs straddled a pile of suitcases on the floor. As soon as we started a little elderly man nearby spoke to me and threatened to become chatty. I looked straight at him with what I thought was a little smile, but was probably more like a foolish grin to him, and said nothing. When he persisted I repeated my formula about being deaf.

He turned away to find another audience, whom he amused by making jokes at my expense, all of which, of course, I had to ignore. He was a mean little man and I would have loved to wring his neck. The train stopped at every station and the journey seemed endless. I had memorized all the larger stations so that in the event of a hasty detrainment I would know where we were in relation to other places and to the frontier. I ticked them off as we passed: Modena, Parma, Piacenza, Lodi – they came and went horribly slowly. From the beginning I had prayed that if we had to run for it we would at least be over the river Po; at last we crossed it. The heavy rain beat drearily across the Lombardy plain. Every stream was in spate, in every hollow lakes had formed; the Po itself was wide and muddy.

In the corridor there was an air of jollity and no one seemed to resent the overcrowding; on the contrary, they enjoyed it. Near the door was a ladies' toilet and as we progressed the women in the carriage kept coming down to it, squeezing past everyone with the greatest difficulty. One cheery old fellow installed himself as doorkeeper and as one woman came out he would call: 'One more!' If a lady overstayed a period he thought reasonable he would knock on the door and urge her to hurry. Everyone enjoyed him. As each woman passed me at my corner I had to crouch to make room and this brought my weight down on the cases below me. After a while I saw my troublesome old man look down intently. He struck a match to see better and held it near my feet. I looked down and a dreadful sight met my gaze. My weight had split two or three cheap cases from top to bottom and out of the cracks appeared ladies' lingerie, gloves, etc.; worst of all, there was a sickly red mess on the floor that was either red wine mixed with mud or strawberry jam – the match went out before I could decide. My position would have been bad if the old man

56

or anyone nearby had been the owner and involved me in an argument of which the results could only have been disastrous. I prayed hard. The old man looked at me and winked. obviously the bags weren't his. I determined to be well out of the carriage by the time the real owner could get to them.

At Lodi, the last stop before Milan, a nice-looking young woman and her husband got in – I don't quite know how they did it. Anyway, she was full of personality and in a very few moments she was the centre of much chattering. She seemed to be re-telling some joke the old man was making at the expense of Lodi, and tried to draw me in to the talk. I smiled back weakly, and the old man came to my assistance:

'It's no use talking to him. He's deaf. Anyway, I think he's a German.'

CATAPULTING FROM COLDITZ

P. R. Reid

Colditz Castle was the famous prison where the Germans sent all those prisoners who were known to be escapers. The author of this account, Peter Reid, was one of those escapers. In Colditz he was a member of the Escape Committee and was one of the people who managed successfully to escape from the Castle and to make his way to freedom. Here, he describes the ingenious method used by one of his fellow-prisoners who also made a successful escape from Colditz.

Lieutenant Mairesse Lebrun was a French cavalry officer, tall, handsome, and debonair, and a worthy compatriot of that famed cuirassier of Napoleon whose legendary escapades were so ably recounted by Conan Doyle in his book, *The Adventures of Brigadier Gérard*.

Lebrun had slipped the German leash from Colditz once already by what seems, in the telling, a simple ruse. In fact, it required quite expert handling. A very small Belgian officer was his confederate. On one of the 'Park' outings the Belgian officer concealed himself under the voluminous folds of a tall comrade's cloak at the outgoing 'numbering off' parade and was not counted. During the recreation period in the Park, Lebrun, with the aid of suitable diversions, climbed up among the rafters of an open-sided pavilion situated in the middle of the recreation pen. He was not missed because the Belgian provided the missing number, and the dogs did not get wind of him. Later he descended and, smartly dressed in a grey flannel suit sent by a friend from France, he walked to a local railway station and proffered a hundred-mark note at the booking-office in exchange for a ticket. Unfortunately, the note was an old one, no longer in circulation. The stationmaster became suspicious and finally locked Lebrun up in a cloakroom and telephoned the camp. The Camp Commandant replied that nothing was amiss and that his prisoner complement was complete. While he was 'phoning, Lebrun wrenched open a window and leaped out on top of an old woman, who naturally became upset and gave tongue. A chase ensued. He was finally cornered by the station personnel and recaptured. In due course he was returned to the Castle and handed over to the protesting Commandant.

This adventure lost Mairesse his fine suit and found him doing a month's solitary confinement at the same time as Peter Allan.[1]

One fine afternoon we heard many shots fired in the playground and rushed to the windows, but could see nothing because of the foliage. Terrific excitement followed in the German quarters and we saw posses of Goons with dogs descending at the double from the Castle and disappearing among the trees. Shouts and orders and the barking of dogs continued for some time and eventually faded away in the distance.

We heard by message from Peter Allan what had happened. The 'solitaries' – at the time a mere half a dozen – were having their daily exercise in the park, during which period they could mix freely. Being only a few, they were sparsely guarded, though confined to one end of the compound, where the prisoners played football among the trees. Lebrun was in the habit of doing exercises with two other Frenchmen, which included much leap-frogging. Now Lebrun was athletic. It was high summer and he was dressed in what remained to him of his former finery – shorts, a yellow cardigan, an open-necked shirt, and gym shoes – not good escaping clothes, but that was also what he reckoned the Germans would think. While a couple of the latter were lolling rather sleepily outside the wire and looking at anything but the prisoners, Lebrun innocently leap-frogged with the other Frenchmen.

It all happened in a flash. His French colleague stood near the wire and, forming with his two hands a stirrup into which Lebrun placed his foot, he catapulted him upwards. Acrobats can heave each other tremendous distances by this method. Precision of timing of muscular effort is its secret. Lebrun and his friend managed it, and the former sailed in a headlong dive over the nine-foot wire.

This was only half the battle. Lebrun ran twenty yards along the fence to the main wall of the park. He had to climb the wire, using it as a ladder, in order to hoist himself on to the top of the wall which was, at this point, about thirteen feet high. Rather than present a slowly moving target during this climb, Lebrun deliberately attracted the fire of the two nearest sentries by running backwards and forwards beside the wall. Their carbines once fired (and having missed), the reloading gave him the extra seconds he needed. He was on top of the wall by the time they fired again and dropped to the ground on the other side in a hail of bullets as the more distant sentries joined in the fusillade.

He disappeared and was never recaught. He certainly deserves the greatest credit for this escape, which was in the true French cavalry tradition and demanded the very quintessence of courage, remembering the effort was made in cold blood and with every opportunity for reflection on the consequences of a false step. A British officer, in a similar attempt a few years later, was shot dead. The escape savours of a generation of Frenchmen of whom the majority disappeared on the battlefields of the First World War and who, alas, never had the chance to sire and educate a generation like themselves to follow in their footsteps.

The loss, which was so deeply felt in the 1930s and which found physical expression during the critical days of 1940, is happily in these days of the 50s fading like a bad dream. The young blood of France is quickening again and there is a new courage in the air.

I met Lebrun again long afterwards, when the war was over, and here is the end of his story.

Lebrun escaped on 1 July, 1941. Although he had the sleuth-hounds and a posse of Goons on his tail within ten minutes, he managed to hide in a field of wheat. (You must walk in backwards, rearranging the stalks as you go.) There he hid the whole afternoon with a search 'plane circling continuously above him. At 10pm he set off. He had twenty German marks which were smuggled into his prison cell from the camp. He walked about fifty miles and then stole a bicycle and cycled between sixty and a hundred miles a day. He posed as an Italian officer and begged or bought food at lonely farmhouses, making sure, by a stealthy watch beforehand, that there were only women in the house. His bicycle 'sprang a leak', so he abandoned it and stole a second. On the journey to the Swiss frontier he was stopped twice by guards and ran for it each time. On the second occasion, about twenty-five miles from the frontier, he tripped the guard up with the aid of his bicycle and knocked him out with his bicycle pump. He took to the woods and crossed the frontier safely on 8 July.

Within a week he was in France. In December, 1942, he crossed the Pyrenees and was taken prisoner by the Spaniards, who locked him up in a castle. He jumped from a window into the moat and broke his spine on some rocks at the bottom, was removed, laid down on a mattress, and left to die. A local French Consul, however, who had previously been endeavouring to extricate the incarcerated Lebrun, heard of the accident and insisted on an immediate operation. Lebrun's life was saved. He eventually reached Algeria to carry on the war. Today, though permanently crippled by his fall, he is a pillar of his own country.

If any German had examined Lebrun's cell at Colditz when he left for his daily exercise on 1 July, he might have nipped Lebrun's escape in the bud. Lebrun had packed his belongings and addressed them to himself in France. Months later they arrived – forwarded by Oberstleutnant Prawitt, the Colditz Camp Commandant!

Notes
[1]Lieut. A. M. Allan.

TOO GOOD TO BE TRUE

Anthony Richardson

In May 1940, Wing-Commander Basil Embry's plane was shot down over France after a bombing raid. In the book, *Wingless Victory*, Anthony Richardson tells the story of Sir Basil Embry's journey across occupied France and back to Britain. Here he describes how Sir Basil Embry was twice captured by German soldiers and how he escaped from them.

At a quarter to twelve he was crossing a clover field. The ground was undulating so that only when he reached the crest of one of the small ridges was his field of vision sufficient to see any distance ahead. Far off, the line of the downs rimmed the sky and it seemed to him that nothing lay between him and that far-distant horizon but mile upon mile of grassland.

It was while he was traversing one of the shallow inclines and wondering how long it would be before he saw the farm which he had promised himself to see, that he heard the unmistakable sound of an approaching lorry. He was so astonished that he halted in his tracks, amazed.

The sound grew louder. So still was the air that the vehicle might have been some miles away, but when he started on his way again and reached the higher ground he saw the truck about a mile off, driving directly at right-angles to the line of his set course. That there was a road beneath him was now obvious, though hidden in a fold in the ground. What was just as obvious was that the occupants of the lorry might have had him under observation for the last five minutes. And he was sure that they were Germans, for he could, he thought, just discern a steel helmet on the driver's head. He was caught in the open and their paths would cross.

His first impulse was to drop flat but he realized at once that the very action would be suspicious. He thought then of changing his course so that they should have passed by well before he reached the road. That again could arise suspicion. The third course would be to bluff it out – to tramp on unconscious of anything so commonplace as a lorry on a road. He knew at once the latter was the only thing to do.

It was quite impossible to regulate his own walking speed in relation to that of the lorry so that he could be certain of their not meeting together at the point of crossing. The contours of the ground hid the vehicle momentarily and it was clear the road took sudden turns. He decided to cross if possible ahead of the truck. But the lorry was carrying on fast with an open road ahead.

He crossed the road without looking to either side. He could hear the lorry roaring and clattering along on his left as he reached the grass verge and made his way resolutely up the slope that led to the next ridge. At every pace he expected to hear a challenge but the sound of the lorry's progress continued and he was already a good thirty yards on the western side of the road, when all of a sudden the sound stopped.

It stopped to the accompaniment of screeching brakes and a bellowing voice. Embry turned in his tracks and stood stock still.

There were five of them. One steel-helmeted, the others in forage caps; four German troopers with an *unter-offizier* in charge. The latter carried a tommy gun, the others had unslung rifles.

They came up the slope at a brisk pace, their weapons at the ready and still shouting. Embry walked towards them. If there were a part to be played it must be played in earnest and with precision. This was the moment he had dreaded. Now it was upon him and his wits were with him. He attempted a smile.

'Who are you?' The *unter-offizier*'s French was only just adequate.

The German was on a level with him now. He was a tall young man, weedy rather than thin and like his companions burnt deeply brown with the sun. The rest of the party were all of a kidney, lean, aggressive and very truculent. Embry could almost see the unmistakable aura of the hooligan about them. These were not the young soldiers of Guderian's Panzer divisions nor the men who had stood beneath the trees of the wood near St Omer. These were the spawn of the Nazi Youth Movement, the little Hitlerites, the bullies and tormentors.

'Who are you?'

'Je suis Belge,' said Embry.

'That is a lie. You are a soldier.'

'No. A Belgian. A refugee.'

'You lie. You are an English soldier.'

He was not expecting to be kicked. The *unter-offizier*'s toecap caught him on the thigh. The blow was too low for his groin but it sent him staggering. One of the Germans gave a sudden laugh. A strange sound, beginning and ending on the instant, bestial, maniacal. A blow from a rifle butt across his shoulders sent him spinning towards his interrogators once more. The *unter-offizier* seized him by the lapel of his ragged coat.

'You are an English soldier in disguise.' His breath smelt of garlic.

'No,' said Embry. 'I am a Belgian.'

He thought to himself: 'I must keep my temper. Whatever they do, unless they intend to finish me right off, I must put up with it. I've got to play the part I've chosen.'

'Where are your identification papers?'

'I lost them on the way.'

The *unter-offizier* threw back his head. His teeth were large and yellow but very even. 'He lost his papers,' he said in German. 'He says he lost his papers on the way.'

They shouted with laughter and one of them brought the heel of a rifle butt smartly into Embry's ribs. For several seconds he could scarcely see for the nausea from the pain. Then he knew they were searching his pockets. They tore the neck of his flannelette night shirt and tugged at the belt of his trousers. They found the pocket-knife and the spoon and fork which he had taken from the French farm and threw them away, though, for a reason never to be known, they left his watch. As they searched and pulled him this way and pommelled him that way, as if he were a rag doll torn by puppies, they gabbled in excited German like little mad dogs yapping.

The *unter-offizier* ordered his men aside and completed the search in an official manner, now that the lads had had their fun.

'No papers. Nothing to identify yourself with. And you still say you are Belgian?'

'Yes,' said Embry stoutly.

'We'll soon find that out. But if you are English . . .' He drew his hand across his throat.

'Now you come with us.'

A kick on the flank helped Embry on his way. They reached the truck and he climbed in while they mounted guard over him, then they in turn clambered in and ranged themselves on either side of him while the driver took his seat. They drove off.

His back was sore and his ribs were aching, so that it was painful to breathe freely. He felt stunned and baffled by this preposterous turn of his luck. It wasn't as if he'd walked into a trap. His captors could claim no credit for their prize. The merest mischance had thrown him into their clutches. A few hundred yards one way or the other across the downs or along the road and he would still have been tramping over the grass and not crouched, bruised and beaten, on a wooden seat in a jolting truck filled with vicious young enemies.

They had turned from the main road by now and taken a secondary road to a small bridge hitherto concealed by a high shoulder of the downlands. Embry could see, as they ran down the incline, the slate-grey roofs of the houses amongst the shrill green of the trees in their early summer foliage. Within minutes they were driving through a gateway opening into a farmyard.

There was a hayrick in the far corner and a large manure heap in the centre of the stable yard. There were farm buildings on either side and the farmhouse stood on the right. It was a bleak, drab little place with the paint of the front door peeling and blistered. They all leapt out and Embry followed them.

He got down slowly because his ribs and back were sore from his thrashing, so that the *unter-offizier* shouted at him again, while a trooper flung open the front door. Someone struck him as he went in and he stumbled but they pushed him down the corridor on the ground floor. There was a room at the far end on the left and they thrust him in, slamming the door on him, but only after the *unter-offizier* had said:

'If you do prove to be an Englishman, we shall shoot you.'

He sat down in the far corner opposite the door, with his back to the wall in just the same way he had sat in the cottage in Dreuil Hamel an hour before dawn of this selfsame day. There, dispirited and disillusioned, he had communed with himself, fighting down all weakness of the flesh, commanding himself to step forward once again. But now all his resolutions and efforts had been in vain.

The long night marches through the crops, the rivers he had swum, the swamps he had plunged into and struggled through, the starvation and the thirst, all had led but to this.

There was, of course, a limit to all things. There was no sense in pretending there was not. There was so much that could be demanded of a human soul and no more. Now he could only wait for the end.

An hour passed. Now and again he heard German voices and footsteps outside. He made no attempt to try the door or to unfasten the sash of the one window. Any attempt to escape by that means would be not only too obvious but would prove the falsity of any story he might contrive. He must carry through the farce. He must bluff his way through. But what use now to keep the sorry half-hearted act alive?

He was as certain it was the end as he had ever been about anything. They didn't believe his story. He had no means of supporting it. They had only to get an interpreter to interrogate him and his deception was revealed. They wouldn't keep him here after dark because the room was insufficiently secure. Even if he continued to convince them he was Belgian, they still would have to deal with him. Therefore before dark they'd have to make up their minds what to do. He had no illusions on that point.

They were going to shoot him. This was to be the dirty, disgraceful end, bullied and beaten and shot to death by little German corner-boys.

In the instant the wrath rose in him. It rose from the humiliation of his shameful treatment. It rose in a flame of indignation. He said, 'By God' – and he meant 'By God' – 'If they're going to do this to me, then someone's going to pay for it!' As always, although fury seethed within him, his brain became icy clear and he knew what he would do. And this was the time to do it, because between two and three of an afternoon was a bad hour with Germans who were accustomed to overeat and drink at their midday meal.

He went across the room and kicked the door. He kicked it three times, savagely, viciously. The sound of the kicking went down the corridor, filled the house. Then he shouted and ran back to his corner opposite the door and crouched down. He heard approaching footsteps and let his head sag forward as in assumed exhaustion and let his arm lie limp at his side. The door opened.

He saw that the young German who entered was much of a height with himself but probably a stone lighter, a clean-shaven pimply-faced young man of about twenty-two, unsavoury, unremarkable. His rifle was slung over his shoulder and his lower lip protruded moistly. He advanced to the middle of the room, his hand ready on the rifle sling. Embry touched his own lips with his left hand, gestured as if raising a cup with his right.

'Thirsty,' he said in French.

The German shrugged his shoulders and strode out of the room. Embry rose to his feet. He leant against the corner, half-huddled there, in all appearance a broken figure, lamed and suffering. He could hear the faint sound of a pump being used in the yard outside. The room was stiflingly hot with the heat of the afternoon sun but it was not only the heat that made the perspiration run down Embry's face and trickle to the corner of his mouth. The door opened again and the young German soldier reappeared. He held a cup half full of water in one hand, the other was still on the sling of his rifle. He advanced casually, a look of curiosity on his face as if he were inspecting some caged animal. He held out the cup.

Embry hit him. He hit him with all his strength and skill and the timing was perfect. His knuckles met the German's jaw with a click and the German's head went back and his legs gave way. Embry kicked him in the stomach before he reached the floor and when he was down he kicked him again. He could have torn the fellow's throat out even if he were dead because he was berserk, mad. He snatched up the man's rifle from the floor where it had fallen and made for the door.

Embry ran out into the corridor and at the far end he saw a second German on guard just inside the threshold of the front door. He was wearing a forage cap and had his back to Embry and leant upon his rifle and Embry was down the passage before he could turn. Embry lifted the rifle he had seized, swiftly reversed it and brought the shodden heel of the butt down with a terrible blow on the crown of the sentry's head. The man went slithering to the doorstep till he collapsed in a heap with his head at a ludicrous angle on his shoulder. Embry leapt over him and sprang into the yard, He heard the clanking of buckets and the sound of somebody whistling a musical comedy sort of air. The sound came from his left. A third German in shirt-sleeves, carrying a bucket of water in each hand, rounded the corner of the house. Embry leapt at him.

The whistle faded from the German's parted lips and, even as he struck, Embry could have laughed at the look of astonishment and pained bewilderment on the other's face. But the brass-plated rifle butt, swung at arm's length, took the German on his left temple and he and the buckets went asprawl. And Embry said: 'Crikey! But I'm building up a score!'

He looked around him wildly, frenziedly. No one was watching from any of the windows. There was no one, it seemed, in the small barn and outbuildings. No one came running and shouting. No one fired a shot. But he couldn't stay here in the broad daylight of a June afternoon in the bloodstained stable yard of a French farm with victims, such as these, for company. He made up his mind at once. He would hide on the spot.

He looked round desperately. Somewhere not very far away he thought he heard the sound of a car. He flung the rifle away, ran four paces and dived head first into the manure heap which was in the middle of the yard.

It was a large manure heap, some forty feet across. The weeks of fine warm weather had dried the dung and straw so that he managed to burrow his way down easily, clawing out the manure in great handfuls till he lay at the bottom of the heap. As he had burrowed down, so the straw had fallen into the cavity he had made, covering and concealing him. He felt that, provided no one had seem him make the initial plunge, he would be completely safe till nightfall.

He lay listening but there was no sound of human movement from the yard beyond. It was hot and steaming at the bottom of the dung pit but he lay utterly still, not daring to shift his position. So the long afternoon and evening passed, the hours dragging slowly by. Once or twice he thought he heard the rumbling of transport along the adjacent road, but the sound died as quickly as it had come and all that remained was the buzzing and murmuring of innumerable insects busy amongst the ordure over his head.

It was just after eleven o'clock that night that he crept out of his hiding-place. He extricated himself with the utmost caution, moving only a foot at a time until his head and shoulders were clear.

The stars were out in a clear sky. He could see the unlit farm buildings across the yard and peered anxiously through the darkness to see if the body of the third German whom he had attacked had been removed, but he could disinguish nothing in the lower-level darkness of the yard.

He was clear of the heap within minutes and crawled on all fours as close to the ground as he could in a direction away from the buildings. His progress was slow, even slower perhaps than his passage across the lawn on the night he had fought and climbed the holly hedge, but at last he found a taut length of wire barring his passage and knew he had met a boundary fence. He pressed his way through, only once pausing as a strand of wire beneath him flew back into the position from which it had been forced with a reverberating twang that sounded to him like the booming of a 'cello. But the silence flowed round again as he waited and he knew he was as yet undetected. He crawled on.

He continued his passage on all fours for two hundred yards, and with every yard forwards his spirits rose. In this crazy 'through-the-looking-glass' world into which he'd been projected a mood could change within minutes. He should by all the laws of chance have been dead by now, but he was alive and he had taken toll of his enemy.

He rose to his feet and looked about him. He appeared to be in open country, a continuation of the downland he had crossed in the morning, though here and there he could discern small patches of woodland on the long slopes of a hillside or a clump of trees on the hillock of a ridge. The stars were still bright and clearly visible. He picked out his old and faithful ally the North Star, took his bearings and strode away to the west.

He reached the village of Huppy well before dawn. He could tell almost at once by its air of quiet solitude that it was deserted. In common with so many other of the senses that his present predicament had quickened he was coming to recognize the emptiness of a place instinctively as soon as he reached it. He walked boldly forwards, well satisfied with the ten miles of downland he had left behind him and desperate for food.

He tried two houses without any success. He would, he knew, have to deal with this question of hunger very shortly, else all the good fortune which had now swung in his favour would be lost. Also he must rest. He tried a large house, further down the street, and entered it.

In the living-room he found, as he had expected, letters and cards giving him his position; and in the kitchen, in the corner, a large earthenware crock. He raised the lid, peeped in, sniffed.

His nose indicated a possible find. The smell was very faintly rancid but not over-pungent. He put his hand in and extracted a cold and greasy lump. He took it to the doorway and under the starlight saw that it was a piece of very fat pork. He nibbled at it and though it was very stale and unpalatable, his stomach cried out for more. He took another mouthful, laid the precious remains on the table and went in search of what further he might find. His luck was holding.

There was cider in an outhouse adjoining the scullery. There were three great tuns on their wooden jigs and each was broached and tapped. He sampled a mouthful or two, catching the liquor in a cupped hand. It was strong and clean to the palate. He looked round for a bottle and to his delight discovered two on a window ledge behind him. It was still quite astonishing how the acquiring of the simplest articles in existence could become priceless and miraculous. He filled the two bottles, collected his piece of pork from the kitchen and left by the back door as dawn was preparing to break.

There was a meadow behind the house with an unthatched haystack in the far corner. He walked blithely and light-heartedly towards it. A happier hour was upon him. He had in his hands food and drink and ahead a resting-place which he badly needed; and although it was a struggle to reach the top of the rick and though he must needs delay his meal till he had removed all traces of his footholds on its sides, nevertheless in a little while he was securely ensconced in the couch in the hay which he had made for himself; and a bottle of cider and a piece of half-rancid fat were alternately at his lips. Things were certainly on the mend.

He left Huppy on the following night, having decided,

in the light of his recent experience, not to walk, for the time being at any rate, by day.

He left at the usual time, striking off again westerly, finding to his infinite satisfaction that the country was still open. Obstructed no longer by high crops and woods, he made, with the short grass of the downlands beneath him, the excellent progress of twelve miles, and just before dawn of 11th June he entered the outskirts of Dargnies.

He took an immediate fancy to the farm with the corrugated Dutch barn which confronted him. Though he knew by instinct the place was uninhabited, it possessed a more ample, prosperous appearance. The straw and hay were stacked high beneath their shelters and two cows roamed in the yard. Moreover, judging by their lowing and the tension of their strained udders, they were unmilked. He felt he must bear that in mind. Then he saw the nesting-boxes ranged round one side of the spacious yard.

Several of the nests contained eggs and he collected over half a dozen of them, which he carried into a dairy adjoining the farmhouse. The grey slate shelves were clean and unstained and the many vessels of polished tin and earthenware hanging on their hooks were as bright and shining as they might have been in any Devon farm. Between a separator and a churn in the centre of the room stood several buckets, scoured and bright. He picked up two of them and returned to the yard. This was an occasion to do things in a big way.

He had no difficulty in milking the cows. He used one bucket for a seat and the other one soon sang to the rhythm of the squirting milk. Indeed from the experiences of country boyhood he appreciated the pain unmilked cattle could endure. It was, he felt, eminently satisfying to do both himself and the cows a good turn. In a little while he had nearly half a bucket full. He returned to the dairy.

He chose an enamel dipper from the row of vessels, broke six eggs into it and poured in a pint of milk, still warm and frothy. It was a drink fit for a giant. He went into the house.

The sun was now well up but so greatly was his confidence renewed that he felt he could afford to be bold and take his leisure. The style of the place was quite definitely superior to those of his previous visitations. If there were a certain homeliness about it, there was at the same time the suggestion of some solid worth. The living-room approached more to the level of a dining-room than a kitchen; the small sitting-room rejoiced in mahogany and brass; and in the hall, with its black-and-white tiles, a noble grandfather clock still ticked.

He opened the front panel of the clock and saw the weights were about half-way down. The owners of the place could not have left long. That, no doubt, was why the buildings and their surroundings still carried the air of cheerfulness and warmth which he had first noticed.

It was while he was by the clock that he experienced that first spasm of giddiness which was to re-occur so often. At the same time he felt a constriction in his groin, hitherto unnoticed. It was as if already at the first signs of relaxation, the physical aspects of his predicament must assert themselves. His leg was beginning to hurt abominably but he continued his search through the rest of the house.

He found all necessities of the table and filled his pockets with spoons and knives and forks. He discovered, moreover, much to his relief, another map, and what was to prove more useful, a penknife. Then he went into the garden and picked some strawberries and lettuce and, satisfied that nothing more could be done for the moment, chose a ladder from several propped up against the stanchions of the Dutch barn and climbed aloft.

It was excellent accommodation. The hay was dry and

sweet and there were several sacks to be found, piled in the centre. The roof immediately above was corrugated iron as opposed to murky and cobwebbed rafters and there was, therefore, less chance of spiders and earwigs dropping down between the collar of his scarecrow jacket and the flannelette nightdress. He made his couch and laid out his provisions. There was the pork – a trifle more greasily repulsive in the daylight perhaps, if that were possible – some eggs – impeccable dish, even if taken raw – strawberries, no need to be over-critical of the greenness – and lastly the lettuce, and if the outer leaves were full of grit then the centre was clean and juicy, and what was a caterpillar or two among friends? Add to all this, fork and spoon as befits a gentleman, and a bottle of sharp, sour, good country cider to wash it all down. What more could any man desire?

After he had eaten he took down his trousers and examined his leg. Maman Paul's bandage was now a thing of the past. His leg was very swollen and all around the small wound the flesh was purplish and inflamed, the skin tight stretched and glistening over a swelling. He examined his groin, and found that the glands in the crutch were swollen and extremely painful to the touch. He realized that the limb, if left untreated, might develop septicemia or gangrene. He knew no more of practical first aid or elementary medicine than any other man brought up and trained in his particular Service, but common sense told him that a mere flesh wound would not produce a state as serious as this. Either through the vicissitudes of his enforced journey through marsh, slime and mud, infection had entered, or in the first place the wound contained some foreign body driven in by the explosion of the shell that had blown in the window of his aeroplane. He took out the penknife from his pocket and opened it.

It appeared to be a comparatively new knife, its blade bright and clean, its edge and point sharp. He tried it with his thumb. It seemed adequate for the occasion. He held it firmly between two fingers, cut firmly and deliberately a quarter-inch incision over the swelling.

The pus spurted out, yellow and noisome, and the glistening tight lump of the swelling became flaccid. He waited several seconds as blood trickled down to his knee and then he squeezed the wound gently till it was rid of its purulence, washing it clean with water from the bucket which he had carried into the loft. He saw the cause of the trouble.

There were two specks of perspex embedded in the flesh. He could see them clearly as he trickled water over the place; he recognized them for what they were at once, remembering the near-miss that had smashed in his side window. It was two small fragments of the splintered window which were causing the festering. He marvelled that two such morsels could make such trouble, poisoning the whole thigh. The matter, however, must receive attention. With finger and thumb he pressed the side of the wound and the two fragments came away.

He stayed in his bunk of hay for twenty-four hours, scarcely moving but to take a drink or break an egg and eat it. His leg still hurt very badly but the swelling in his groin seemed to have subsided a little and the thought that the origin of the trouble had been removed was a rare consolation. At one of the periods between the familiar snatches of sleep he studied his newly-found map and came to the conclusion that he was certainly not less than ten miles from the coast. He could, he felt, now that his goal was in sight afford to rest awhile and conserve his strength, for the task ahead might even necessitate rowing across the Channel and the perils of the sea were even greater, he supposed, than those of the land. Therefore, he consoled himself with conceiving various plans, though very little, he realized, could be decided upon before he was actually on the coast and could assess the facilities available. He would, though, collect all the food possible within the next day or two, carrying it with him against the prospect of a prolonged voyage at sea. Thus, with the pain of his wound gradually abating, he sank with quietude and some measure of contentment to sleep.

In accordance with his plan, after he had descended from his couch the next morning and milked the two cows, he set about collecting what food might remain, to furnish the reserve which he had decided was essential. He made a tour of the nesting-boxes and collected no less than thirty eggs. He carried them cautiously to the dairy and placed them on a shelf taking a pride which he knew was laughable in ranging them in straight rows. When the pattern was complete they looked very well. He was quite delighted with it and now that he felt so much better in health, delighted also with himself.

He returned to the house with the idea of discovering something in which to carry his possessions, a bag or a cloth or a pillow-slip. He found nothing suitable downstairs so went above, choosing a room overlooking the main street. While he stood by the window, staring down, interested in viewing the village by daylight, two men came striding down the street.

They were tall and young with sticks across their shoulders, carrying bundles of their belongings. They walked erect and with a swinging gait; two carefree, well set-up youngsters, whom he was sure were British soldiers in disguise as French peasants. They were past him before he could hail them, swinging by the front of the house and down the main street at a fair steady pace.

He ran downstairs and out of the house at once, determined to overtake them, if only to warn them of that soldierly way of walking of theirs, which was bound to betray them. Even so, in his eagerness to meet with them, he himself nearly forgot to assume his customary shuffling gait.

78

But to his surprise he found after several minutes of walking that they were not alone in the street. Other people were beginning to appear. There was a small group further along by what appeared to be a church, and a woman with a child in her arms was trying the lock of a cottage opposite with a key. The villagers were beginning to filter back, so that it seemed to Embry that the Germans must have advanced even further than he had imagined and that, although he was so near the coast, the area would be well in the rear of their armies and therefore practically unmolested. Therefore, he quickened his pace, more anxious than ever to overtake those two, who, combined with him, might make a useful crew in a sizeable boat, to say nothing of their companionship. He was almost on the point of breaking into a run, being not more than twenty-five yards behind them, when the German patrol appeared out of a side turning.

Indeed so swiftly was he moving, so intent on his purpose, that he practically stumbled into the two young men with their sticks and bundles. The German patrol – an *unter-offizier* and three men – halted the young men and on the instant Embry could thank his stars he had not been able to catch up with them. He had no taste for interrogation with what lay in the yard of a farm some few miles away near a manure heap. So, at once, he side-stepped as if to move past the group, wondering even at a moment so tense as this how the devil he was going to get back to his precious collection of eggs without hindrance; but even as he was passing them by there came the well-known guttural shout for him to halt. He turned and faced them.

The two young men were already moving off under an escort of two Germans. The *unter-offizier* and one trooper stood before Embry and the former looked him up and down before he said: 'We want you, too. Come along.'

Embry wondered, for one desperate moment, if he could succeed in dashing up the side street and dodge amongst the lanes till he reached open country again; but the *unter-offizier*'s hand was on his belt where his holster was strapped, so Embry shrugged his shoulders and without another word they led him away. He wondered what they knew of him and what they might have heard. There was an empty feeling in the pit of his stomach.

Fifty yards further down the street they turned into a house on the right. There was a noticeboard in the passage and printed papers hanging in a clip from a nail. Here, clearly, was German local headquarters. He passed through a door on the left and was at once before the German Intelligence Officer.

The room was bare with a table only along one wall and another running across the window overlooking the street. The Intelligence Officer with an *unter-offizier* sat at the first table, a clerk sat at the other. The escort stamped, saluted, turned about, and left the room.

'Your identification papers, please.'

The Intelligence Officer's French was perfect. The two young men searched in their pockets, produced their identity forms and handed them across. Embry stood aside and knew that he had only a few brief seconds to evolve a plan before his own turn came.

It would have to be a very good plan. It would have to show a little more forethought than he had revealed in the last twenty-four hours. He was face to face with the enemy once more.

There could now be no dash down a corridor with a swinging rifle butt and Germans going down like ninepins all around. There could be no leaping to safety as he had leapt from the ranks of the Calais column under the very muzzles of the machine-guns; here was to be no battle with fists and broken heads, but a cold duel of wits. And all the time the coast was only ten miles away.

The Intelligence Officer was talking, snapping out his questions and in French, as good as his own, the two young men were answering back confidently and accurately. And Embry thought: 'The seconds are passing and I haven't got a plan. For God's sake let me have a plan.' He thought again: 'I can't be a Frenchman now for my tongue will betray me at once. I can't be a Belgian, because in a nearby town there is a Belgian with a beard and a ragged coat who is wanted for assault if not murder. What the hell, then, can I be?'

The seconds passed and the Intelligence Officer handed their identity cards back to the two young Frenchmen. Embry thought: 'I've got it now. They spoke the truth. So will I. I'll be myself. I'll be an Irishman.'

'Very well. You may go.'

The two Frenchmen went out.

The Intelligence Officer raised his head in Embry's direction. He was a thin, handsome fellow of some twenty-five years; a cool cultured young man, correct in his manner.

'Your identity papers, please,' he said in French.

'Les cartes d'identité, s'il vous plaît.'

Embry shook his head. The Intelligence Officer rapped on his desk.

'Tout de suite, les cartes.'

'Cartes – non,' said Embry.

'Mais, ce n'est pas possible . . .'

He broke into a rapid torrent of French, making his points with a darting emphatic finger. Even if he had been a fair French scholar the speed of the other's delivery would have baffled Embry. He allowed the flood to envelop him for several seconds, then he waved the German into silence.

'Too fast,' said Embry in his own particular French.

The Intelligence Officer attacked from a fresh angle.

'Who are you?' he asked in English. He spoke with a strong accent but with copy-book clarity.

'Non,' said Embry unconcernedly.

'Who are you? Where do you come from?'

'Non savvy.'

'Can . . . you . . . speak . . . English?'

'Engleesh,' Embry grinned. 'A leetle . . . yes-no?'

He thought to himself: 'It's all in the balance. He's watching every move. This man knows his job.' It was blade to blade and riposte to the parry.

'Sprechen sie Deutsch?'

Embry shrugged helplessly.

The Intelligence Officer leant back in his chair, turning to his *unter-offizier*. They spoke rapidly together, throwing a gesture from time to time to the clerk at the far table. The Intelligence Officer took up the interrogation again. His attitude was full of suspicion, his look intent, his eyes fast on Embry's face; the spider in the centre of the web, ready to scuttle across its net and seize its fly; the cat crouched ready to spring on the mouse.

'What is your country?' he asked in French.

'Non savvy,' said Embry.

'Le pays . . . Oh, mon Dieu . . . what a fool is this fellow! Le pays . . . quel pays . . . ?'

'No good,' said Embry.

The Intelligence Officer broke into English again.

'What country do you come from?'

Embry shook his head. He thought to himself: 'I can't go on playing dumb much longer. If I tax his patience too far, they'll have to find some way of getting rid of me that will probably be the local gaol pending inquiries. I don't like the idea of inquiries. There's probably a description of me already being circulated to all headquarters within fifty miles of the farm where I bumped those Jerries off.'

The Intelligence Officer muttered, swearing in German:

'Donnerwetter – Mein Gott in Himmel.'

He snatched a sheet of paper from his blotter and wrote the same question in capitals: 'What is your country?'

'Ah,' said Embry. 'Give me.'

He took the pencil from the German's hand and drew the sheet of paper towards him. He made the rough sketch swiftly, the cross he added last:

The cross was practically correct for Galway. It was a point to be maintained. The *unter-offizier* took the paper from Embry, studied it and then held it triumphantly beneath his superior's nose.

'So,' he said to Embry, 'you are English after all?'

'Non,' said Embry.

'But you see,' said the Intelligence Officer. 'This cross shows it.'

'Not English,' cried Embry, 'Irish!' he shouted. He struck the table before him with a clenched fist. 'Irish . . . me! English . . . merdes! Bah! L'Angleterre – fineesh! To bloody hell with England!'

He leant across the table till his face was only inches from that of his interrogator.

'You call me Engleeshman, I spit on you! England – no damn good. Engleesh . . . salous! Me – Irish. Sinn Fein. IRA. Republican. You tell *me* – me – English . . . !'

He shook his fist in the Intelligence Officer's face. The German laughed; he threw back his head and laughed like a boy, showing his teeth and half-heartedly fending Embry off. Embry was nearly across the table and the ink bottle was on its side and the ink was running over the papers on the blotter and still he shouted, till the clerk from the other table sprang from his chair and seized him by the arm. The *unter-offizier* joined them and he, too, was laughing. He patted Embry on the back and dragged him forcibly to the centre of the room. There he calmed him down, explaining that no insult had been intended, that it was merely a question of establishing identity and nationality came first. Still Embry protested, sulking, muttering to himself. To be taken for an Englishman! To be mistaken for one of those swine!

'Calm yourself,' said the Intelligence Officer in English. 'Sit down at this table. We will talk.'

The clerk brought him a chair. Embry sat down opposite the Intelligence Officer and because the initiative of the moment at any rate was his, he opened his mouth and pointed to it and champed his jaws to show them that he was hungry. He thought: 'If they bring me food, it will delay the interrogation and I can hold it up from time to time if I'm in a tight corner, and the more time I have, the better my story will be.' Moreover, his hunger was real and to order food was a sign of his own ability to control a situation where a single false move would mean the walk to the roped stake and the firing squad.

The clerk fetched a loaf of bread and a tin of jam from an adjoining room and Embry tore at the loaf with his teeth like a wolf and dug out the jam with his dirt ingrained fingers so that his beard became dusty with crumbs and clotted with the droppings of the jam. The young German officer looked away with distaste. It seemed to Embry that the act was going very well indeed but somewhere, sometime there would be a trap laid. He must go very warily indeed.

'Now,' said the Intelligence Officer. 'Let us continue.'

They went about the task with the help of pencil and paper and by making themselves understandable to one another in pidgin English and broken French.

He was an Irishman, Embry told them, one time member of the Republican Army that had fought against the English. He had carried out a great deal of sabotage, indeed, in England itself; he had been one of the most active members of the IRA, putting acid in letter-boxes amongst other things. He was particularly proud of the work done actively in England. It had been carrying the fight to the hated enemy's own front door. At this there was an opportunity for a little more fist-shaking.

He was then put in gaol, he continued, for his activities, but he'd escaped, beating up one of the English warders on the way out. Just before the war he had gone to Belgium.

'Whereabouts in Belgium?'

'Brussels,' said Embry promptly.

'Your occupation?'

'Washing up in a café.'

He felt he had navigated that passage reasonably well; but he told himself, there still could be a trap. He must keep alert.

'Continue with your story.'

'Story's the right word for it,' thought Embry, and readily continued. Yes, he'd worked hard in the café because he'd wanted to save enough to return to Ireland, to his wife and family. So he had a wife, had he? Indeed, he had. And her name? Maureen, begorra. But he hadn't seen her for months now. The war had overtaken him, the café was no more and he'd been driven south with all the rest of the refugees. And that was that.

They took it all in. The *unter-offizier* nodded his head from time to time in intelligent sympathy, but the

Intelligence Officer tapped his notes with the tip of his pencil. Then he asked quietly:

'What language did you speak in Ireland?'

'Erse,' said Embry, who had not spoken one word of Erse in his life.

'You don't speak my language, or French, or English at all well. But I expect you speak your own.'

'Of course,' said Embry and knew at once that he was in a corner.

'Speak to me in your own language, then.'

'Burra-pag jeldi karo,' said Embry without a moment's hesitation, speaking Urdu. 'Dawazer bund karo!' (Hindustani for 'Bring me a large whisky and soda' . . . 'shut the window.')

The Intelligence Officer grunted. He raised his eyebrows to the *unter-offizier*, who nodded. They seemed well satisfied.

'Who is in charge of the Irish Army?' said the *unter-offizier*.

'Michael O'Leary,' said Embry, making up the first name that came to mind. 'Surely you know that?' he added. 'A very famous soldier was Michael O'Leary,' said Embry. He added that he thought everyone would have known that. Of course they knew it, the Intelligence Officer replied testily. Certainly they themselves knew all about O'Leary, they'd wanted to know whether Embry did, that was all. Was this O'Leary married?

'Twice,' said Embry, quite confident in creating a family background for a personality who only existed in his own imagination.

'There was a divorce?'

'No. A motoring accident. Like the Queen of the Belgians. Very sad.'

They agreed. Very sad indeed. 'And this,' said Embry to himself, 'is where I take these silly clots for a ride.'

'When will you win the war?' he asked.

'We've already won it,' said the Intelligence Officer.

'That's good,' said Embry. 'Now I can go back to my wife Maureen and my children in Ireland.'

The Intelligence Officer shook his head. 'No. We shall send you into Germany.'

'I don't want to go to Germany,' said Embry, speaking the truth for a change. 'I don't want to go to Germany at all. Why do you want to send me? You have won the war, you tell me, and I tell you I have fought the British, so we are comrades – friends.'

'You would only be there for a short time.'

'But why send me at all?' There was nothing like pressing home the attack when the initiative was his. 'Why not put me on a German ship,' he said boldly, 'and send me to Ireland? That's the thing to do.'

The Intelligence Officer considered the proposal. His attitude was one of official but sympathetic interest.

'In time we will find some way to send you back.'

'But I don't want to wait,' said Embry. 'I have wasted weeks as it is.'

'We will see.'

'Let me find my own way then. Let me get to Spain and there I'll find a ship.'

'How did you get here?'

'From Brussels. I walked by night and laid up by day.'

'How did you get over the Somme? All the bridges that were not down were watched.'

'I swam it.'

The two Germans conferred together. Embry sat at the table and waited their verdict and felt like a schoolboy in the headmaster's study.

'We must refer the matter to higher authority,' said the Intelligence Officer. He laid his pencil on his blotter and picked up a sheet of paper.

'But why must I wait?' said Embry.

'Take him away,' said the Intelligence Officer in German.

The *unter-offizier* took Embry by the arm. He led him across the room and across the passage to another very similar room beyond. There was a mattress on the floor, the German indicated it with a jerk of his head and went out, slamming the door.

Embry lay on the mattress and attempted to sort his thoughts out. One thing seemed palpably clear. There could be no half measures on this matter. Either he had succeeded or he had failed. Either he would live to continue on his way or he would die almost at once. It was as simple as that.

What was not so simple was to determine the next move. He was not to all appearances closely guarded and it might just be possible to make a dash for it. But this house was without doubt a headquarters and there were bound to be Germans in plenty in the immediate vicinity. If a breakaway succeeded, well enough; but if it failed, it would be utterly fatal. The bottom would be knocked out of his story. They'd start to work on him again, possibly check back on facts and in the end he might break down. No, better the present anxiety and suspense than to take as great a risk as that. In the vernacular, that was his story and he was sticking to it.

But the map was still in his pocket and it occurred to him that an Irish dish-washer would scarcely have even the elementary skill to read a map, far less set a course by it. He took the map from his pocket and ate it.

That is to say he ate half of it, but finding it extremely unpalatable, pulped the other half only and pushed it into the mattress. Thereafter he stretched himself out and tried to rest.

But it was difficult to relax. The shock of this second recapture had come so rapidly upon the other. He wondered with what sources the German Intelligence Officer and his staff were getting in touch; no doubt they would check up with similar local administrative establishments throughout the whole neighbourhood. It was going to be a near thing. The door opened and a German sentry came in.

The German was young with a pimply, spotted face, like that first of Embry's victims, but white where the others had been sunburnt brown. His shoulders sloped, even the rifle on its sling looked too heavy for him. A sallow, pallid, undergrown young man, who with Embry's fingers round his throat would have snapped like a reed. But Embry refrained, because he had resolved on a course of action and, come what might, he must keep faith with himself.

'Come with me.' said the sentry and turned his back and went out, so that for one wild moment Embry must struggle with himself to prevent the leap forward and the flailing arms but he followed the young German down the passage and out into the yard at the back. He thought: 'So this is it! This is where they do their shooting.' Then the German pointed to the pump.

He was watching Embry curiously, an uncertain uneasy look of the half-scared and Embry, not understanding in any way but with the certainty that death was not far off, could only spread his hands and mutter: 'Ne savez pas'. The German picked up an enamelled mug from the foot of the pump, filled it and handed it to his prisoner.

Embry drank and handed back the cup. He asked:

'What are they going to do with me?'

For reply, a shrug and a shaking of the head and then the German's thumb inclined towards the gates of the yard. They went out side by side and turning right met the main road of the village. They walked briskly with Embry shuffling along as well as he could. As they progressed the certainty of his own approaching end increased. It was as he had surmised; they had been on the telephone and got the description of the wild-eyed tramp who'd done the job down the road. And it fitted. That was how he put it to himself. This was definitely the end. They wouldn't have shot him in the yard of the headquarters anyway. It was too much in the middle of the town and the German tactics were clearly to handle the civil population as gently as possible. Therefore he was being taken to a nearby wood, some sheltered glade, probably even now littered with corpses, the recognized shooting gallery of the local German administration. On the other hand, why the friendly gesture of a cup of water, and why only one man to escort him to the firing squad? Or was it to be a one-man job, a short order and a shot in the back? Whatever answer there might be to this confused problem, one point was apparent. He was quite equal to dealing with the youngster at his side, armed though he might be. Very well then. He would fix him.

Sooner or later, he told himself, they would have to leave the main street and branch off down a side turning. That would be the moment to tackle his man. There were too many people about in the main road. Then he realized how many more people there were than there had been an hour before.

They turned from the street and took another, narrow and twisting a way through the ill-assorted buildings. Here, at any moment would be the place for his attack but there were still people about. They were gathered at the doors of the cottages and at their garden gates; they were lounging against walls and the women chatting together, while the children tugged at their skirts. The village was returning to life.

This was deplorable. In all other circumstances he could have rejoiced but now he could never have raised a hand but he would have been seen and the alarm raised. He must walk like a sheep to the slaughter-house. Then they were through the outskirts of the village before he realized it and had halted in the middle of the road. On all sides the open country rolled away in bare downland.

They stood face to face. The German's rifle was slung

on his shoulder. He looked very frail and irresolute. There was nobody in sight now.

'Go,' said the German, and he pointed where the road curled away to the north-east. 'Go,' he said again.

Then despite himself, Embry grinned, because this was too good to be true. But 'Go' the little German sentry said again and turned away. Then the hand that a few seconds before would have been at the escort's thin throat was upon his sloping shoulder.

'Germans very good people,' said Embry.

'Au revoir,' said the little German soldier and turned about and marched back along the road towards the village.